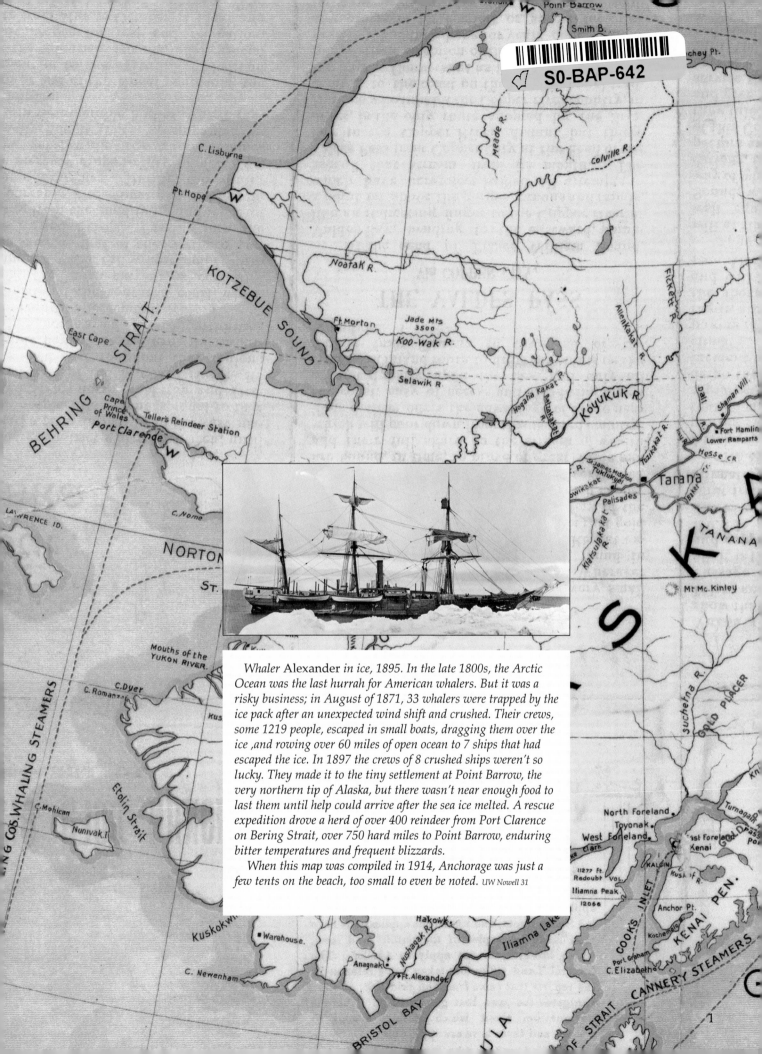

Whaler Alexander in ice, 1895. In the late 1800s, the Arctic Ocean was the last hurrah for American whalers. But it was a risky business; in August of 1871, 33 whalers were trapped by the ice pack after an unexpected wind shift and crushed. Their crews, some 1219 people, escaped in small boats, dragging them over the ice ,and rowing over 60 miles of open ocean to 7 ships that had escaped the ice. In 1897 the crews of 8 crushed ships weren't so lucky. They made it to the tiny settlement at Point Barrow, the very northern tip of Alaska, but there wasn't near enough food to last them until help could arrive after the sea ice melted. A rescue expedition drove a herd of over 400 reindeer from Port Clarence on Bering Strait, over 750 hard miles to Point Barrow, enduring bitter temperatures and frequent blizzards.

When this map was compiled in 1914, Anchorage was just a few tents on the beach, too small to even be noted. UW Nowell 31

A favorite from my collection of historic Alaska photographs is this scene from Port Clarence, near the Arctic Circle, circa 1900. In the distance are seven steam whalers (two are behind the tent on the left) and two smaller schooners, the latter probably used for trading. You can clearly see six of the protected barrel-like crow's nests on the masts of the whalers.

In the foreground are two canvas tents next to a kayak, its hull made of caribou or seal skin stretched over a drift-wood frame. Standing on the left-hand tent frame are what appear to be hoops of seal skin or perhaps whale blubber drying. On the post are some carved ivory figures.

There are few protected harbors in northwest Alaska, and this one on the Seward Peninsula not far from Nome was a favorite anchorage for whalers. UW NA2125

2017 Edition

Coastal Publishing
15166 Skogen Lane, Bainbridge Island, WA, 98110
Printed in the United States

Maps by Joe Upton

Photographs by Joe Upton unless noted with the following abbreviations:
AMNH - American Museum of Natural History, New York
AM - Anchorage Museum
AS - AlaskaStock
BCARS - British Columbia Archives and Records Service
BCRM- British Columbia Royal Museum
CRMM - Columbia River Maritime Museum, Astoria, Oregon
DK - Dan Kowalski
MOHAI - Museum of History and Industry, Seattle
SFM - San Francisco Maritime Museum
THS - Tongass Historical Society, Ketchikan, Alaska
UAF - University of Alaska, Fairbanks
UW - University of Washington Special Collections
WAT - Whatcom County (WA) Museum of History and Art

ISBN 978-0-9887981-7-5

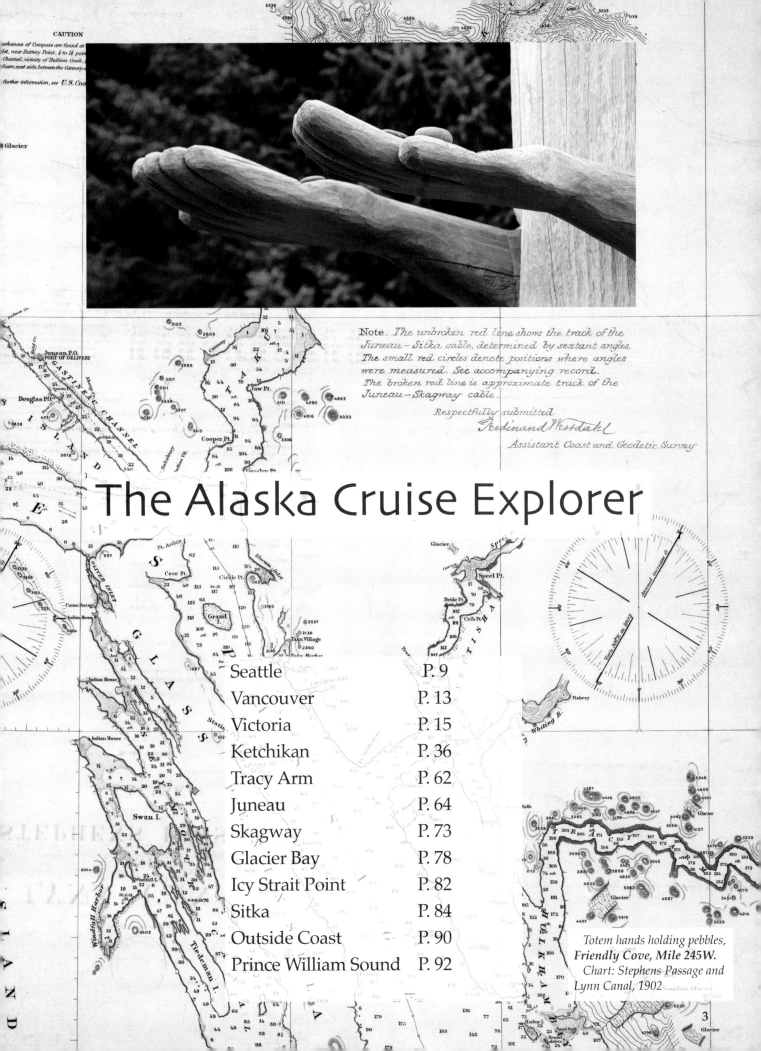

Note. *The unbroken red line shows the track of the Juneau–Sitka cable, determined by sextant angles. The small red circles denote positions where angles were measured. See accompanying record. The broken red line is approximate track of the Juneau–Skagway cable.*

Respectfully submitted

Ferdinand Westdahl

Assistant Coast and Geodetic Survey

The Alaska Cruise Explorer

Totem hands holding pebbles,
Friendly Cove, Mile 245W.
Chart: Stephens Passage and Lynn Canal, 1902

3

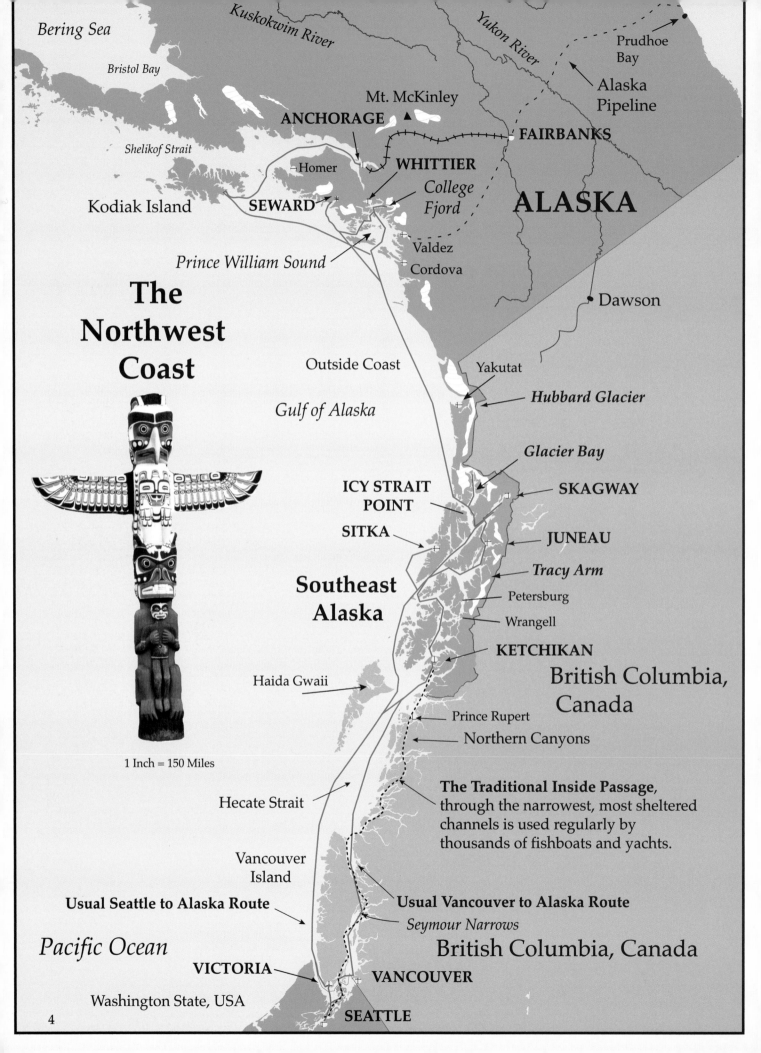

Bering Sea

Bristol Bay

Kuskokwim River

Yukon River

Prudhoe Bay

Alaska Pipeline

Mt. McKinley

ANCHORAGE ▲

FAIRBANKS

Shelikof Strait

Homer

WHITTIER

College Fjord

ALASKA

Kodiak Island

SEWARD

Valdez

Cordova

Prince William Sound

Dawson

The Northwest Coast

Outside Coast

Gulf of Alaska

Yakutat

Hubbard Glacier

Glacier Bay

SKAGWAY

ICY STRAIT POINT

SITKA

JUNEAU

Tracy Arm

Southeast Alaska

Petersburg

Wrangell

KETCHIKAN

Haida Gwaii

British Columbia, Canada

Prince Rupert

Northern Canyons

1 Inch = 150 Miles

Hecate Strait

The Traditional Inside Passage, through the narrowest, most sheltered channels is used regularly by thousands of fishboats and yachts.

Vancouver Island

Usual Seattle to Alaska Route

Usual Vancouver to Alaska Route

Seymour Narrows

British Columbia, Canada

Pacific Ocean

VICTORIA

VANCOUVER

Washington State, USA

SEATTLE

Mickey Hansen and me, Southeast Alaska, 1965. He showed me the ways of The North and filled my head with wonderful stories.

Mile 30 ▷

Look for these video icons in this book and on our maps. They refer to our 3-5 minute mini-documentary videos that we have created at specific places along the Inside Passage. They may be seen on the video page of www.joeupton.com.

Our map and navigation system: this book is designed to be used in conjunction with our illustrated **Alaska Cruise Map**, available on Amazon and on many ships. Ship routes are shown with numbers based on a "Seattle is Mile Zero," system. Many ships use this system to announce ship position, such as "We are now at mile 522 on your map."

When I was a green kid of 18, I had a powerful experience—working my first Alaska job on a fish-buying boat, delivering salmon to a remote Native-owned cannery. Mickey Hansen, the grizzled Norwegian mate who had worked 50 seasons "up North," took me under his wing and shared with me the lore and legends of this vast region. That kindly old man was full of wonderful stories: "We went in there in the old *Mary A*, winter of '31. Thick o' snow, we'd toot that horn and listen for the echo off the rocks, through the snow." In this way, he gave me a passion for The North that I still have to this day.

For twenty years, I worked the coast in all kinds of boats, in all kinds of weather. I was a fish-buyer, a salmon fisherman, a king crab fisherman decades before "The Deadliest Catch."

When the wind blew, the anchor would go down and the rum bottle and the stories would come out.

When the big cruise ships started coming north, I designed a series of books with illustrated maps to share with these new visitors the drama and beauty of The North.

A few years ago, I started working with commercial fisherman/filmmaker Dan Kowalski. We'd take his boat to remote places and film short stories about what had happened there.

For me, the books and maps at first, and later the videos, were a way to share a sense of the mystery and the power of this place that is such a big part of my life.

So, come take this journey through a land that remains much as it was when the first explorers came through.

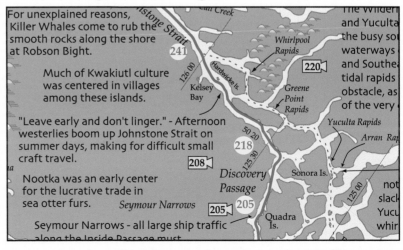

For unexplained reasons, Killer Whales come to rub the smooth rocks along the shore at Robson Bight.

Much of Kwakiutl culture was centered in villages among these islands.

"Leave early and don't linger." - Afternoon westerlies boom up Johnstone Strait on summer days, making for difficult small craft travel.

Nootka was an early center for the lucrative trade in sea otter furs.

Seymour Narrows - all large ship traffic along the Inside Passage must

Mile Zero *of The Inside Passage begins in Seattle at Colman Dock. Look for the big ferries; they carry 2000 passengers and 220 cars from busy downtown Seattle to rural Kitsap County.*

Mile 2 - *Akli Beach... It was here that Seattle's first settlers, slogged ashore in a rainstorm in November, 1851. The women of the party, who'd spent the previous six months struggling with the rigors of the Oregon Trail, broke into tears when they saw the promised land: a roofless cabin at the edge of a gloomy forest.*

Less than a month later, the sailing ship Leonesa *dropped anchor, and her skipper offered the party $1,000 cash for a load of 50-foot fir piles. The settlers sharpened their axes and an industry was born.*

When English explorer George Vancouver sailed into Puget Sound in the spring of 1792, he was stunned by its beauty and promise. Today, much of that promise has been fulfilled as the land has filled up with people, homes, and businesses.

First was the lumber business. When the first settlers arrived, little did they know that the just starting California Gold Rush was the beginning of a seemingly insatiable demand for timber that could only be satisfied by the kind of good harbors and vast stands of timber that was the hallmark of Puget Sound. Axes echoed in the woods and steam whistles called the men to work in ports up and down the sheltered waters of the lower Inside Passage, as an industry was created that dominated much of the 20th century, and remains important in the 21st.

Next came manufacturing, primarily aircraft as Boeing became the largest airplane maker in the world, dominating the employment scene as well as keeping literally hundreds of small operations busy making parts for the big jets.

Then this college dropout named Bill Gates came up with this language for operating computers and the high tech industry that was to eventually rival aircraft manufacturing, began rolling. Next, this guy Howard Schulz had the crazy idea that he could create worldwide demand for his brand of coffee and the shops that sold it. Another entrepreneur, Jeff Bezos, had this really out there idea of an online store that would sell you almost anything.

Turned out that their ideas weren't that crazy after all, and by the time 2015 rolled around, Microsoft, Amazon, Starbucks, Google, and other high tech companies were on the way to transforming Seattle into the third fastest growing city in the US.

Those who came for work found plenty to like: mild climate, thriving arts and music scene, spectacular scenery and wilderness close at hand.

Top: 14,409' Mt. Rainier looms near Seattle.
Right: Big square riggers loading giant Douglas fir timbers on Bainbridge Island around 1880. SFMM F12.21.725n

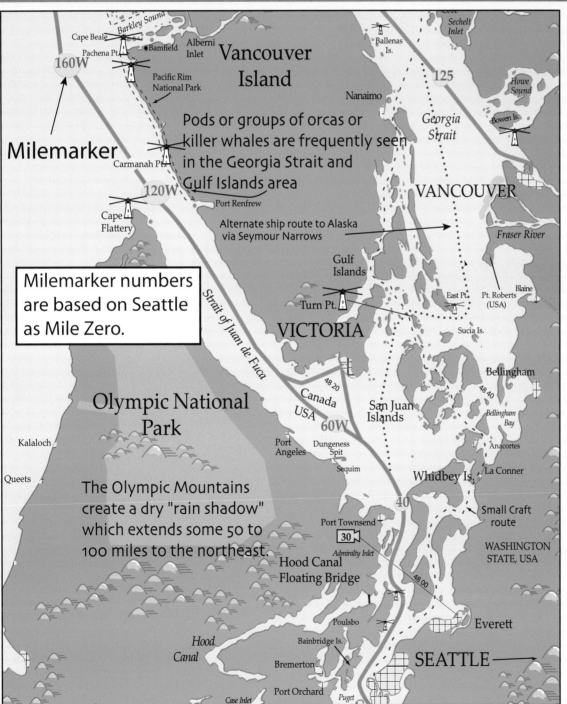

Milemarker

Barkley Sound

Cape Beale
Pachena Pt.
160W
•Bamfield

Alberni Inlet

Pacific Rim National Park

Vancouver Island

Nanaimo

Carmanah Pt.

Pods or groups of orcas or killer whales are frequently seen in the Georgia Strait and Gulf Islands area

120W

Port Renfrew

Cape Flattery

Alternate ship route to Alaska via Seymour Narrows

Ballenas Is.

125

Georgia Strait

Howe Sound

Bowen Is.

VANCOUVER

Fraser River

Pt. Roberts (USA)

Blaine

East Pt.

Milemarker numbers are based on Seattle as Mile Zero.

Gulf Islands

Turn Pt.

VICTORIA

Sucia Is.

Strait of Juan de Fuca

48 20

Canada
USA

San Juan Islands

Bellingham

48 40

Bellingham Bay

Olympic National Park

Kalaloch

Queets

60W

Port Angeles

Dungeness Spit

Sequim

Anacortes

La Conner

Whidbey Is.

Small Craft route

The Olympic Mountains create a dry "rain shadow" which extends some 50 to 100 miles to the northeast.

40

Port Townsend

30

Admiralty Inlet

Hood Canal Floating Bridge

48 00

WASHINGTON STATE, USA

Hood Canal

Poulsbo

Bainbridge Is.

Everett

Bremerton

SEATTLE

Port Orchard

Case Inlet

Puget

Mile 14 - Kingston Ferry, *one of the four major routes that take thousands of workers every day to work and home across Puget Sound.*

Mile 19 - Possession Point: *over the bluff east of here is the Boeing Co., airline builder to the world.*

Mile 25 - Foulweather Bluff *is the entrance to Hood Canal, home to the Pacific nuclear sub fleet and one of many bridges that sank or blew down. The present Hood Canal bridge was rebuilt after its predecessor sank in a 1979 windstorm.*

Mile 30

Mile 38 - Port Townsend *with Victorian homes overlooking the water is a center for arts and crafts and especially the building and care of wooden boats.*

Mile 40 - Point Wilson *is the lighthouse on the point and marks the transition between the calmer waters of Puget Sound and the rougher waters beyond.*

Mile 50 W - Sequim Rain shadow: *The high ridge of the Olympic Mountains serves to scrape the rain out of the storms sweeping in from the Pacific Ocean, creating a much drier and sunnier climate here.*

Exploring:
The Wild Olympic Peninsula

Mile 60W: *Orcas are often seen in these waters, particularly along the Vancouver Island shore.*

Mile 80W: *Olympic National Park occupies much of the Olympic Peninsula south of here.*

Mile 90W: *A spot known as "one square inch of silence" is hidden in the Ho Rain Forest south of here. I is believed to be one of the quietest places in the continental U.S.*

Mile 120W: *Cape Flattery is the most northwesterly corner of the continental U.S. The coast to the south of here is remote and rugged.*

Top and far right: Second Beach, La Push, WA
Right: Ocean Shores, WA.

Wild is almost too tame a description for parts of the Northwest Coast. With very limited road access, long sections of the coast are totally isolated, only accessible by hiking through rough and thick forest. Nor are these shores particularly friendly when you actually get to them. In many places stretches of beach are cut off from the next beach by cliff-like headlands. At high tide, there may be no beach at all, but rather a jumble of driftwood that often includes large logs and whole trees, moving and surging with the waves that roll into it, creating a place where beachcombers could easily be injured or crushed.

There are spectacular hikes, particularly in the Hurricane Ridge area of Olympic National Park, south of Port Angeles. Farther west are some dramatic beach hikes. Shi Shi, near Neah Bay, and Rialto or First or Second beaches near La Push are accessible and very scenic.

8

Pike Place Market is probably the most varied food and craft market on the West Coast. It has several great places to eat overlooking the sound. Exciting!

Pioneer Square: This area of First Avenue at the southern end of downtown is an eclectic collection of galleries, shops, ethnic restaurants, the excellent Gold Rush Museum, and lots of street art. The highly recommended Seattle Underground Tour begins just off the square.

Seattle Art Museum: On First Avenue, in the heart of downtown, the museum just finished a major renovation. It offers many permanent and rotating collections. Highly recommended.

Fishermen's Terminal & Ballard Locks: Much of the Alaska fishing fleet, including some boats seen on "The Deadliest Catch," are based here.

Waterfront & Aquarium: Seattle's waterfront is a hopping place, a collection of shops, restaurants, and docks for excursion vessels. The Blake Island tour with a salmon dinner and Native American dancing is highly recommended. The latest addition to the waterfront is a large Ferris wheel with enclosed cars. If you ride on it in the long summer dusk, you'll get a super view across Puget Sound to the Olympic Mountains which rise to almost 8,000 feet.

Museum of Flight: Located next to Boeing Field, between downtown and Seattle-Tacoma International Airport, the museum features recent additions of stunning WWI and WWII dioramas.

Seattle Center: A popular attraction is the Experience Music Museum with its wonderful historical exhibits and hands-on activities, including an excellent section on Seattle's own wild and groovy Jimmy Hendrix. Another must-see attraction is the IMAX film of the Mount St. Helen's eruption, which shows several times a day at the Pacific Science Center.

Walk on the ferry: The Bainbridge ferry departs from downtown frequently during the day offering a 35-minute ride across Puget Sound. A 10-minute walk on the other side takes you to the pleasant village of Winslow.

A few well-regarded restaurants in Seattle are: Ivar's Acres of Clams, on the waterfront; McCormick & Schmick's, 1103 First Avenue; Anthony's Pier 66, waterfront; and Dragonfish Asian Cafe, 722 Pine Street.

Exploring:
San Juan Islands

"A place in the San Juans" is the ultimate dream for many Northwesterners—a little waterfront bungalow somewhere among the large and small islands of this sleepy archipelago, just 60 miles north of Seattle. With four major islands served by ferries out of Anacortes, and dozens of smaller ones, the San Juans are a major destination for vacationers and urbanites with second homes here.

Washington State has an excellent system of marine parks throughout Puget Sound and the San Juans, some on roadless islands with no ferry service. Many, many Washingtonians got their first taste of the islands as youths in one of the many summer camps, and just kept coming back as adults.

Above: A "Waterfront fixer-upper?" In your dreams! This is a cabin at Camp Four Winds on Orcas Island.

Left: guitar maker and dealer at an island craft fair.

Above: tanker and connected tug in Rosario Straits. Here the shipping channel is so narrow that Coast Guard regulations require tankers to be escorted by tugs that with a towline attached so as to be immediately available in case of engine failure or other emergency.

With increased oil production from the upper US midwest and Canadian oil sands, tanker traffic through these islands is forecasted to increase substantially, with several proposed oil terminals in the works. These are treacherous waters with swift tidal currents, and many groups are concerned about tanker safety even with tough regulations.

Just acoss the border with Canada, the Gulf Islands spread along the west shore of Georgia Strait. Served by numerous ferries, this sleepy archipelago is especially popular with boaters seeking a less crowded experience than in the islands south of the border.

The largest and probably busiest (and trendiest) island is Saltspring, where as one visitor observed, "every other house offered either massages, yoga lessons, or homemade yoghurt."

As in the American San Juan Islands, a number of parks allow boating visitors a semi-wilderness experience. Naturally, many boaters seek this out and in many anchorages, vessels are encouraged to drop their anchor and then tie a sternline to a tree. This provides a more secure mooring while also allowing more vessels to fit into narrow and long anchorages.

Top: satisfied skipper aboard his elegantly restored six-meter yacht, Saskia.
Right: ferry leaving the Thetis Island dock for nearby Kuper Island, and then on to Chemainus, on Vancovuer Island in the distance.
Above: your author and mapmaker exploring at Tumbo Island Marine Park. ML Upton photo.

Like most Northwest coast cities, forest products played a huge part in Vancouver's history, with big square riggers waiting to take lumber to Asian, Australian, and Pacific ports as soon as it could be milled. It still continues today – you'll cross the Fraser River entering the city by bus or car. Look down and most likely you'll see BC's premier product, logs, (some say marijuana is the biggest export...) traveling by barge or raft to a sawmill or a waiting ship.

With one of the best harbors on the coast, good road and rail connections, Vancouver quickly developed into Canada's premier west coast port as well. With a dramatic mountain and waterfront setting, the city became one of the favorite spots in the British Empire within a few decades of being founded, as evidenced by the many large and elegant Victorian era homes.

In more modern times, concerns about what would happen in Hong Kong after the mainland Chinese took over in 1997 led to the arrival of large numbers of Chinese immigrants, many of whom brought substantial personal wealth with them. The result is a noticeably multi-ethnic city with the second biggest Chinatown in North America.

Early Vancouver planners had the foresight to create Stanley Park, along the waterfront and close to downtown. Within walking distance of Canada Place, the main cruise ship terminal, it is a elegant place to explore and enjoy.

Aquabusses along the waterfront take travelers back and forth. An excellent aquabus destination for a meal, shopping, or just to explore, is Granville Island.

Opposite page top: Early morning cruise ship approaches Canada Place.
Opposite middle left: Freighter and First Narrows Bridge
Opposite right: Shopping on Granville Island
Above: Tug and log raft, Vancouver, circa 1880. John Horton painting.
Left: Totems, Stanley Park, near Canada Place.

Exploring:
Victoria

While Vancouver—just 75 miles to the northwest—is a modern, cosmopolitan city with a heavy sprinkling of Asian immigrants, Victoria seems more like a taste of Olde England. The British fondness for gardens is especially evident in the many private and public gardens and plantings that line its streets.

Originally settled around a Hudson's Bay Company trading post established in 1843, this city and Vancouver Island became a crown colony in 1849. Ten years later, another colony was established on the mainland to support the many prospectors who had arrived with the 1858 Fraser River gold strike. Eventually the two colonies merged to form what is today British Columbia. Victoria became its capital, while Vancouver became the industrial center.

Victoria is a good place to shop for First Nations (coastal native) art and craft souvenirs. Many shops also specialize in goods from England that are hard to find elsewhere.

Because there are often orca or humpback whales in the vicinity, fast whale watching boats leave regularly from along the waterfront. Twelve miles from downtown Victoria is Butchart Gardens, one of the most popular attractions in the province. This stunning 50-acre showpiece had a rather humble beginning. In 1904, Jennnie Butchart, whose husband operated a nearby cement plant, got tired of staring at the ugly scar that his limestone quarrying operations left. She brought in a few plants to spruce up the area and one thing led to another.

Also downtown across the street to the south from the big Empress Hotel (where the afternoon tea is an elegant ritual), is the excellent British Columbia Provincial Museum. Behind it to the east is an excellent totem pole display, open around the clock.

Opposite page: The Empress Hotel dominates the Victoria waterfront.
Top: Totem near the Provincial Museum
Left: Statue in Butchart Gardens

"April 29, 1792. At four o'clock [a.m.] a sail was discovered to the westward standing in shore. This was a very great novelty, not having seen any vessel but our consort, during the last eight months."

THE EXPLORER

Mile 160W: *The Bamfield Cable Station was where the undersea telegraph cable to Australia entered the ocean.*

Mile 195W: *The many inlets and sounds in this area and farther north have become a major center for fish farming, employing many commercial fishermen looking for work after wild salmon runs declined in the 1980s.*

Mile 220W: *Nootka was a native village, home to the Nuu-chah-nulth people, where Britain and Spain agreed to a peaceable settlement to their conflicting territorial claims on the Northwest Coast.*

Top: A painting by John Horton depicts Captain George Vancouver about to enter the Strait of Juan de Fuca.

Right: Part of Vancouver's map. Note that Glacier Bay (red circle) is mostly absent. It was full of ice!

Mile 195E

This was a singular day for the British Captain George Vancouver and his two ships and crews. They had sailed from England to seek the Northwest Passage from the Pacific to the Atlantic.

The sail was Captain Robert Gray, a Boston fur trader, who pointed the way. Soon after, Vancouver discovered a channel 10 miles wide and 500 feet deep, leading east between high, snowy mountains. He thought it was the Northwest Passage. It wasn't.

At that time, Philadelphia and Boston had cobblestone streets and daily newspapers, yet the known world ended west of the Missouri River.

A week after entering the unknown strait, the Vancouver party, continually charting and exploring, following the shore to make sure they missed no channel that might lead to the Atlantic, turned south and entered an unknown waterway Vancouver named for one of his lieutenants, Peter Puget. Vancouver was stunned by the beauty of what he saw.

When he arrived in Puget Sound and saw the myriad channels and passages leading off in all directions, it was obvious to Vancouver that the task of exploring was too difficult for his cumbersome ships, the *Discovery* and *Chatham*. The solution lay in using his 20-foot cutters, rigged to row and sail. The big boats would anchor while the small boats would set out, sometimes with Vancouver and sometimes without, charting the vast land they had discovered.

For three long summers, he explored, naming and charting much of the Northwest Coast. He lost just one man to shellfish poisoning. It was a stunning achievement. He was just 38 years old.

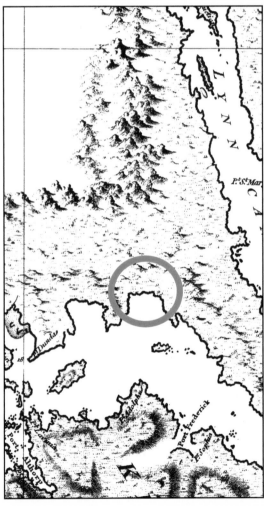

Section of the map explorer George Vancouver made of the Icy Strait area. The circled area is Glacier Bay, full of ice almost all the way down to the entrance. The bay had calved so much ice that Icy Strait was almost impassable.

NORTHWEST TIDES

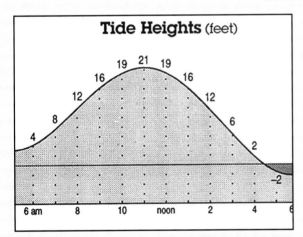

Tide Heights (feet)

21
19   19
16   16
12   12
8   6
4   2
                              -2

6 am   8   10   noon   2   4   6

Imagine this: Several cubic miles of water must pass through the maze of narrow channels north of Vancouver every six hours as the tide moves in and out. This creates violent currents and whirlpools big enough to capsize 60-foot boats! The prudent mariner transits at slack water—near the time of high and low tide.

Once, when I was an incautious young skipper in a 60-footer, I was towing a disabled 36-foot fishing boat from Alaska to Seattle. Eager to get home, but having missed slack water, I thought I could get through constricted Dodd Narrows against the current. So I went up onto the flying bridge and shouldered our way into the stream.

Instantly I knew it was a mistake! The current shoved us violently back and forth and I was desperately afraid that the boat I was towing would hit the shore in one of our wild swings. Finally we got through, and I radioed back to the fellow I was towing, a cool customer, in his 25th season as an Alaska commercial fisherman.

"It wasn't too bad," he answered me, "I had to steer a bit to keep off the rocks. And I bit my cigar in half..."

Top: channel marker near Petersburg in SE Alaska. On a big high tide, the water level would rise to the top of the marker. Six hours later, it would be 20 feet lower. This creates very swift currents, making for some very challenging maneuvering around the cannery docks.

Left, middle: Diagram shows around-the-clock rhythm of the tide.

Left, bottom: This kayaker is surfing on a standing wave in a tide rip at Skookumchuck Rapids, B.C., where the currents rush to almost 20 mph. For a dramatic video of a tugboat capsizing when the current pushes its barge ahead of it, check out: www.youtube.com/watch?v=QEfUblSDzww

We rolled across Georgia Strait, British Columbia, on a late September drizzly Sunday, our chartered 34 footer loaded with kayak, photo and video gear, and most exciting of all, our shiny new Phantom 4 video drone!

Last light found us creeping dead slow into the narrow entrance of Roscoe Bay, with barely enough water under us to slip over the bar. The anchor chain sang its little song and we lit the kerosene lamp and opened the rum to celebrate that exquisite moment, known just to mariners: safe harbor made after a difficult passage.

In the morning we took our drone and launch pad (a 2'x2' piece of plywood) to shore to attempt what we had come so far for: to create powerful aerial footage. But no sooner had we launched it when the video monitor, an iPad 2, flashed a warning: "FIRMWARE UPDATE NEEDED" Quickly landing and back aboard, we discovered that three hours away was a marina that might have wi-fi we needed to upgrade.

Up anchor, down the channel, and YES! They did indeed have wi-fi and we were able to upgrade. Another test flight, up 300 feet, and a quarter mile down the channel, and I hit the 'Return to Home' button, expecting the drone to land within a foot of the spot on the dock that it had taken off from, accuracy that we had experienced in testing. But then: OH NO... as it was descending to the dock we realised at the last minute that it was coming down a few feet over, and headed for the water next to the dock. Panicked, I hit the 'cancel' button, but the 1100$ drone kept dropping while the screen flashed, "Are you sure you want to cancel this action?" By this time it was just three feet over the water, and I grabbed the stick just in time to override the automatic control.

Breathe in, breathe out... I landed the drone safely on the dock and reviewed what had just happened. Changed batteries and up again.. and again, each time without issues, gaining confidence with each flight.

The next evening we lay at the dock at Big Bay, where the current from several cubic miles of water trying to push through a narrow channel swirled around us. The sun dropped over the hills, the light got very dramatic and we launched. Straight up from the dock, higher and higher to the legal limit of 500 feet, and we just stared into the iPad as it displayed stunning images of the land and seascape that mariners had feared and talked about for generations: Yuculta Rapids and the

Drone
landing pad.

Your author,
flying the drone.

sobering whirlpool at Devil's Hole that had sucked down and drowned careless sailors. even flipped over seaworthy 58 footers. All perfectly revealed in the dramatic evening light. I rotated the drone slowly to take in the landscape from all directions, gimballed down to film myself and filmmaker Dan, like tiny dots on the dock far below.

The light began to fade, but only when the low battery warning flashed after 20 minutes, did I reluctantly bring the remarkable little Phantom to a gentle landing on the dock. Put it carefully on the spare bunk, pulled out the micro SD card and loaded it into my laptop. Dan poured us each a glass of a nice hearty box merlot, and we just stared in awe at the images presented on the much bigger screen. Dan and I were both professional photographers, Dan an experienced filmmaker as well. Yet neither of us expected, nor even in the beginning, believed the quality, the clarity, and the crispness of the video: WOW! Now we were ready to get really creative!

The next day we wanted to film our boat as we entered the barely 100 foot wide entrance into Roscoe Bay, where we'd started days earlier but been foiled by the firmware update warning. We stopped a couple of hundred yards off the entrance and launched, the drone following the boat as we went in: totally great footage. Before I landed it, I sent it up to 400' to get a panorama.

But then, just as it was about 5 feet from Dan grabbing it out of the air, another flashing red warning: LOW BATTERY, RETURNING TO BASE, and it shot up to about 100', banked hard and headed back out of the bay to 'home base,' which had been automatically established when we launched, except now we were long gone. Grabbed the stick and brought it back under control.. Breathe in.. breathe out.. this flying drones in the wilderness is not for the faint of heart...

Opposite page top: kayaking around Laura Cove, the setting was so exquisite that it cried for the drone...
Opposite middle: Phantom 4 drone and Ipad 2 monitor.
Opposite bottom: drone view of our chartered trawler as filmmaker Dan gets ready to grab the drone (better than trying to land it when the boat is moving).
This page top: drone on 'launch pad.' Bottom left: drone view of the entrance to Roscoe Bay.

19

Drone landing pad.

Your author, flying the drone.

An hour's steam took us over to Laura Cove, probably one of the most exquisite places in the whole Northwest coast. Plus there was just one other boat there, a very rare event. A month earlier there would have been no place to even anchor; it is extremely popular in summer.

Dropped the hook, launched the kayak, and had barely gotten a hundred yards when I realised we had to get some drone footage - it was just sooo gorgeous. So.. grabbed the backpack full of drone and gear, launch pad, still camera, and piled all into the inflatable. Motored up into this glassy, still cove, found a level place, did all my preflight checks, (propellors on snug, full battery, max altitude & return to base altitude set, collision avoidance on, etc) then it was up and away.

I followed Dan maybe fifty feet behind and forty feet up. Dan's paddle strokes looked like those of a water spider, the bottom was visible under him: just wonderful light and detail. And this was all on the little iPad monitor as I filmed.

Then as he paddled around a corner and out of sight from where I sat, but still visible on the monitor, I applied up stick on the controller, and gimballing the camera down to keep the kayak in view, watched the iPad as the Phantom slowly rose over the tops of the trees, until the kayak was just a dot in this ever expanding landscape.

I kept the camera rolling when I swung back to the tiny cove, the bottom clearly visible, and slowly descended, the amazing camera even catching the waving of the grass around the launch pad before the Phantom touched down!

The next morning was another stunner and I launched again, this time flying around Laura Cove, then following Dan, but this time the images were even richer as there were clouds reflecting with an elegant pattern on the water.

Then sadly it was time to go; we had a full day of 8 knot steaming (7mph) ahead to get back to our charter base by dusk. The rain started again and we realised how lucky we were to have encountered such a window of perfect weather so late in the season!

Opposite top: Dan paddles, Laura Cove, drone is following up and behind him. Middle: Dan and kayak just a dot as I take drone above the trees.

Opposite bottom - view on the way down to land. In this case I am hand flying it all the way down. But in reality the 'Return to Base' feature would do the same thing, except that it would first fly to a position directly over the base (where it took off from) but about a hundred feet up, then it would descend rapidly until about 10' up, then slow until touchdown.

This page top: this is the next morning, still and glassy, but with some clouds to make for wonderful patterns on the water. Dan paddling, lower middle of photo. Photo from about 300' over Laura Cove, wider cove in distance is Prideaux Haven. Right middle: evening light in Laura Cove: not bad..!

Bottom: Dan up on the flying bridge of our chartered trawler as we approach the Yuculta Rapids area from the west.

The Gauntlet - Yuculta Rapids area

It's almost as if nature set a barrier across the route north, right in the spot where civilisation ends and the wilderness begins. As if to say, 'Watch Out, what lies ahead is very different from what lies behind. Be careful.'

Devil's Hole Whirlpool

Dent Rapids

To Alaska

Arran Rapids

Guillard Passage

To Seattle

212 E

Yuculta Rapids

Several cubic miles of water must pass through these narrow passes with each tide change, creating violent eddies and whirlpools. Safe passage is only possible at slack water, and careless mariners have lost their lives here.

No vessel may transit the Discovery Islands area without having to wait for slack water at one of the numerous tidal rapids.

Seymour Narrows the widest, at Mile 205 is used by all large ships.

The main alternate route, much used by yachts and fish boats, is further East, via Yuculta and Dent Rapids, and past the dangerous whirlpool at Devils Hole, Mile 215E.

Mile 205

Mile 212E

There's a sort of invisible line southwest to northeast through the Discovery Islands, from Seymour Narrows in the west to Yuculta and Arran Rapids in the east. Every six hours several cubic miles of water forces itself through these narrow passages as the tides flood south or ebb north.

In each place where the channel narrows, the salt water travels up to 18 MPH. As it passes over the uneven bottom, it creates violent swirls and whirlpools large enough to swallow fifty or sixty footers.

Fortunately, every six hours, at high or low tide, the current briefly stops before reversing and running hard in the other direction. This is **slack water,** which, depending on the size of the tide (which varies with the position of the moon) may last from 20 to just a few minutes. The correct time for slack water, which changes daily, is available in publications known as tide books.

When these strong currents are opposed by the wind, they create dangerously steep and breaking seas or tide rips. The rip south of **Cape Mudge, Mile 195,** is particularly bad when the tide, flooding from the north hits a southeaster blowing up Georgia Strait. Locals call this rip, "**The Graveyard**,"and with good reason. The big tug *Petrel* got into the rip one December night and was swamped so quickly there wasn't even time for a call on the radio.

The rip at Seymour Narrows used to be much, much worse. A ship killer rock lurked right under the surface right in the narrowest part of the channel, skewering numerous ships and creating dangerous whirlpools that swamped many small craft.

Top: Gillard Passage area, drone photo.

Above top: 235' cruise ship Spirit of Endeavor *in tide rip, almost exactly at the 'Mile 212E' icon above. Shortly after this photo the rip heeled the ship enough to sweep bottles and glasses off the bar, cameras off tables, and dislodging one of the life rafts. If the rip had been much stronger she would have capsized.*

Above bottom: the Oosterdam *making the turn in Seymour Narrows.*

Blasting the underwater rock was an immense and hugely challenging project. At first, drillers worked from a barge anchored nearby with four 250-ton anchors! Didn't work. The current was too strong, moving the barge and breaking off the drills.

Finally, a huge tunneling project was undertaken— boring more than 3,200 feet of tunnels and vertical shafts reaching up into the interior of the rock. This was before the invention of sophisticated surveying equipment that we take for granted today. Drillers explored with small-diameter drills until they broke through to the water. Then, they'd plug the hole and use the information to create a three-dimensional map. Finally, tugs brought 2.8 million pounds of dynamite to fill the caverns and, and on April 7, 1958—adios, Ripple Rock!

This gauntlet of tidal rapids also marks another transition - from civilization: noise from the great mills along Georgia Strait, and lights along the shore at night, to the lonely waterways of the North Coast, to bays and inlets that may see months without a human visitor. Even the weather is different - south of Seymour the high mountains of Washington's Olympic Peninsula and Vancouver Island create sort of a rain shadow, the area is even called the Sunshine Coast. But to the north, the land is darker, wetter, cloudier.

South of Seymour is the large town of Campbell River, with hotels, restaurants, boardwalks along the waterfront. South of Yuculta Rapids are big sportsfishing resorts with high rise accomodations, rows of powerful boats to chase king and silver salmon in the rips. But just on the other side of both channels, dark hills rise steeply from the water, houses, even any sign of man's existence at all is hard to find; the difference is stark.

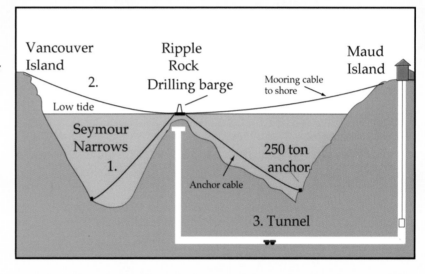

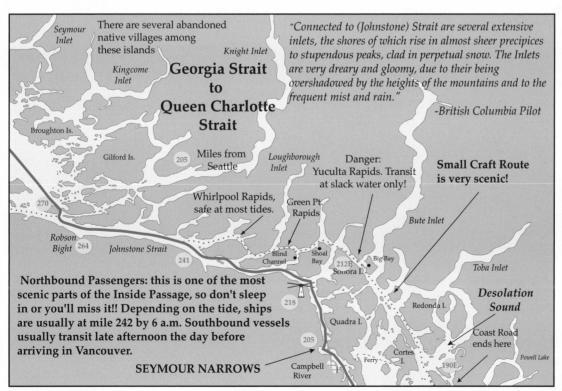

Top: the blast to remove ship-killer Ripple Rock was the largest non-nuclear man-made blast in history. The very difficult tunneling plan was only adopted after multiple efforts to blast the top of the rock off from a barge failed. Even when the barge was anchored with 1,000 tons of anchors, and cabled to shore, the violent currents moved the barge enough to break off the drill bits. As you can see from the drawing, to tunnel down, over, and then up inside Ripple Rock was a masterpiece of engineering, and always with the fear that an unexpected fissure or break in the solid rock would fill the tunnels with water and drown all inside.
Campbell River Museum

The two major lighthouses here are Carmana Pt. at **Mile 125W** *and Pachena Pt.,* **Mile 160W.** *The Shipwreck Trail ran between them.*

Mile 290W: *Cape Cook. More than one couple wanting to head for the South Pacific in their sailboat decided to take a "shakedown cruise" around Vancouver Island. The weather here can be worse than any they would find in mid-ocean, and after a taste of nasty weather, some decided to abandon the whole idea.*

Mile 310W: *Triangle Island was the site of an ill-fated lighthouse built in 1910 on top of a 600-foot cliff. The site proved too foggy and windy. Buildings had to be held down with cables least they be blown off the cliffs. Now home to millions of seabirds.*

The Inside Passage is the collective name for a series of winding channels and waterways, wide and narrow, that allow even very small craft, to travel to Alaska in relative safety.

At a number of places - Juan de Fuca Strait, Georgia Strait, Johnstone Strait, Queen Charlotte Sound, Milbank Sound, and Dixon Entrance, the crossings are exposed enough that prudence dicates that the mariner listen carefully to weather reports. But by doing so, and making sure not to travel through areas where the wind and a strong tidal flow are opposed to each other, even kayakers and rowboats have made it all the way to Alaska.

The smaller a craft is, the more protected channel it will prefer. The traditional route is the one outlined in Captain Farwell's **Hansen Handbook**, a listing of point to point courses that allowed mariners to travel to Alaska without having to buy a stack of charts or expensive chartbooks. However in numerous places, particularly through the Discovery Islands, there are numerous even narrower and more winding routes, like the one above.

It's about 650 miles from Seattle to Ketchikan, Alaska, a journey that would take a typical fishing boat or small yacht, traveling at 8-10 mph a week or longer. Vessels this size typically only travel daylight hours so as to be able to see logs in the water, and anchoring up each night.

Once a vessel leaves the busy Georgia Strait area around **Mile 205**, the trip north is essentialy through wilderness.

Top: Cordero Channel, B.C.
Right top and middle: Grenville Channel, B.C.
Right bottom: would you go to Alaska in this? Such small craft travel every year up the Inside Passage.

So many ships were lost along the west coast of Vancouver Island, that a trail was established for shipwrecked sailors with cabins at intervals stocked with food, firewood and a telephone to the nearest lighthouse.

Tide Rips are area of disturbed and rough water where a strong tidal current flow aganst an opposing wind. The generally occur at the entrances or exits of large bodies of water.

The outside coasts here are very unfriendly places, where most of the time the seas beat upon rocky shores where vessels need to give the coast a wide berth and proceed with caution. Before the wonders of first loran, then radar, and finally GPS - Global Positioning System - that shows a vessel's position as a boat icon on a map on a screen - mariners dreaded the west coast of Vancouver Island and especially the area around the entrance to the Strait of Juan de Fuca.

In those days, navigation was based on celestial navigation - working out one's location from the position of the sun and stars observed with a sextant - and piloting, or simply identifying buoys, lighthouses, or specific places along the shore to track a vessel's position. Many ships, especially sailing ships, approached the coast after a voyage of a month or more across the North Pacific. Typically the closer you got to the coast the more fog and cloudy weather was encountered, with the result that they might find themselves groping through the fog or black of night as they closed with the land.

The effect of the prevailing westerlies and strong tidal currents was to push vessels northwest, toward the unforgiving shores of Vancouver Island with the result that they might find themselves on the rocks before they fully grasped where they were.

Fortunately, big oceangoing tugs often patrolled the area around the entrance to the Strait, asking sailing ships if they wanted a tow into their destinations in the inner waters of Puget Sound or lower British Columbia. At the same time skippers of the big sailing ships wanted to be frugal with the shipowner's money, and often chose to sail on. Sometimes it wasn't a wise choice - by the time the weather had turned, and they needed a tug, the bad weather had driven the tugs to look for shelter themselves.

Top: outlying rocks in the entrance to Esperanza Inlet: not a very nice place..
Bottom: a small freighter rolls along the outside coast near Nootka Inlet.

When your mill leaves town...

Life in Tahsis was prosperous when the mill was going, with good pay, comfortable housing, several restaurants, and a medical clinic.

After the mill closed, the population dropped from around 2000 to less than 400.

For most of the last century if you lived on the west coast of Vancouver Island, you either worked in the woods or on the water or in something that supported logging or fishing. In the early days it was sailing ships that came from Asia for the fish or the timber, then it was the big freighters. If someone had tried to tell a West Coaster it would all go away to be replaced by an economy based on tourism, surfing, kayaking, and tending to the needs of folks from Vancouver and Victoria with second homes there, the reaction would be somewhere between laughter and outright disbelief.

Yet essentially that was exactly what happened. First the pilchards (a herring-like fish) that supported the big cannery and town at CeePeeCee (California Packing Company) in Esperanza Inlet disappeared and it became a ghost town.

Salmon was next; the big runs shrinking from over fishing and damage from logging operations.

"Of course there will be logging forever." Or so went the feeling. But even the great forests and logging operations on the rainy western slopes of the rain forest felt global forces like the impact of digital media on paper needs and the big mills like the one at Tahsis and Gold River shut down, the pieces barged away south or the mill just left to rust while the ships that used to come into load lumber came to load logs right out of the water instead: exporting jobs instead of timber.

But what happened next was totally unexpected: that surfers, kayakers, whale watchers, sportsfishing lodges, fish farms and retirees and wealthy folks with second homes would be enough to create a whole alternate economy.

Places like Tofino, and a lesser degree to Ucuelet and Bamfield, with good road access to Victoria and Vancouver were totally tranformed. Coffee shops replaced machine shops and kayak outfitters replaced fish buyers.

Top: when it closed down, about all that was left of the big sawmill at Tahis was the ramp they loaded the mill equipment onto the barges with..

Middle: loading crew, 1991: these men were proud of their reputation as crew who could put on loads that wouldn't shift or get washed aboard crossing the stormy North Pacific.

Bottom: Tahsis Lumber Co. in better times.

Before the white men came, these waters abounded with sea otters. Unfortunately their pelts (skins) were highly valued in China and the first of some 330 ships began arriving here in 1785. 40 years later the sea otters were almost gone, and most of the natives as well. For as well as merchandise to trade for furs, the Europeans brought disease - smallpox, flu, syphillus, and others - that essentially decimated the natives of the Northwest Coast. As workers returned from cannery and sawmill jobs, walking or paddling back to the most remote villages, they brought the diseases with them.

Top right: inside the Catholic church where native symbols stand amongst the pews, Bibles, and lectern.

Top left: grave marker for a 16 year old.

Left: part of totem overlooking the Pacific Ocean and blackberries taking over a native cabin.

Above: raft of sea otters who have made a huge comeback after almost getting wiped out in the early 1800's.

27

WOULD YOU GO TO ALASKA IN THIS?

Egg Is. Light, Mile 336, was a tough berth. The sea had a grudge - after years of breaking windows and washing away outbuildings, it tried for a knockout blow in November, 1948, sending the lighthouse and keeper's quarters into a roaring sea. The keeper and his family were almost dead when they were rescued five days later.

Mile 310 ▷

Safety Cove, Mile 354, is the traditional spot for southbound small craft to anchor and wait for good weather before crossing Queen Charlotte Sound.

Top: *team Mad Dog Racing, on their way to winning the 2016 R2AK in 3 days, 20 hours, 13 min.* NW Maritime Center Photo.

THE RACE TO ALASKA!

The Course: Port Townsend to Kechikan, 600+ miles up the Inside Passage.

The Rules: no engines, no support vessels.

The Prizes: 1st: $10,000. 2nd: steak knives.

It started, legend has it, in 2014 in a Port Townsend pub: why not have a race to Alaska? Prize: ten grand nailed to a tree. but... no motors... And.. first have a 'qualifier leg' - 40 miles across the often nasty Strait of Juan de Fuca. If you can make it safely across to Victoria, then, you're good to go for Ketchikan after a few days rest.

The word got out and in May of 2015, the strangest fleet began to assemble around the waterfront: big catamarans (with platforms added on the stern to row with **big** oars..!) proas, trimarans, big sailing rowboats, even a windsurfer (that only got as far as Victoria).

Racers rented GPS trackers that enabled race staff as well as internet viewers to follow each boat's progress in real time.

And finally at 5:30 a.m. (to catch a favorable tide) on June 5, they were off! Most made it across the Strait to Victoria for a day of celebrating, vessel repairs, and tuneups, and then on the morning of June 7, the real race began.

As it turned out, the weather for the 2015 race was tough: windy and wet. But 5 days, 1 hour, and 55 minutes later, the exhausted three catamaran sailors on Team Elise Piddock staggered into Ketchikan to claim first prize.

OR THIS?

"**We were laying at Teakerne Arm,** down in B.C., just a ways south of Yuculta Rapids. There were a bunch of log rafts in there so we tied up; we had a couple of hours to kill before slack water. There was a big B.C. troller laying in there and it's owner was just standing on the logs over by his boat, whittling on a stick.

"So I went over for a visit, you know just jawing about the weather and the fishing.. .

"Then there was a sound from the inside of his boat. It was real odd, sounded like a woman crying out in pain or something like that. He excused himself and went back inside and I went back to my own boat. Even from there you could hear some awful moanin' and groanin'. Finally after an hour or so, he came out on the logs again. He was wiping something off his hands onto this old towel. Looked an awful lot like blood.

"So I asked him was everything all right.

"'Aw,' he said, 'we're fine. That was just the baby coming out. It was a little girl."

"**You know how that tide runs there at** Arran Rapids... like it doesn't hardly have any time for slack water - all that water just pushes right up into Toba Inlet and then turns around and runs right back out. Well it was one of them big spring tides and we were laying in there waiting, and there was a half dozen killer whales and a humpie waiting too.. Just about the time the tide stopped and we headed into them Rapids, they did too, like they had a tide table built right into their heads!"

Namu, Mile 374, was the place where a fisherman accidentally captured an orca in his net that became the star of the Seattle Aquarium and changed the way the world perceived killer whales.

Mile 375

Mile 399 - Bella Bella. *Lama Passage,* which starts at *Mile 387,* is one of those places where a fishboat skipper might come forward with a cup of coffee to take over from his crew. This constricted, twisting channel has had plenty of groundings before radar and GPS. The big steamer Mariposa *drove ashore here in the fog in 1915. The passengers were picked up by the next northbound steamer!*

Mile 399 - Bella Bella wharf. This is a small native village and the only settlement for many miles.

Mile 400 ▷

Mile 438 - Boat Bluff Lighthouse - the sharp turn here is difficult for large ships and one of the reasons most avoid this route.

Mile 462 - Swanson Bay - the tall chimney sticking up from the forest is the only sign of B.C.'s first pulpmill and its 500 workers.

Mile 455 ▷

Mile 473 - Butedale Cannery - Boaters traveling at night would be startled to come upon this cannery, the only lights for many, many miles. Sadly, the cannery is slowly collapsing into the bay.

Mile 485 - hidden way up a winding inlet to the northeast is *Bishop Bay Hot Springs.*

Mile 485 ▷

Mile 501 - 546 - Grenville Channel, the narrowest and most scenic part of the traditional Inside Passage. Boats occasionally lay alongside the waterfall at *Mile 521* to fill their water tanks.

The Inside Passage from 30,000 feet

Top: Looking into Grenville Channel from *Mile 501.*

Top lower: the Fraser Reach area of the Inside Passage, around *Mile 468.* Here the channel runs right through the mountain heart of British Columbia.

Above: your mapmaker and his crew at Bishop Bay Hot Springs near *Mile 483.* We stopped here after a long season of buying fish in the 75' fish packer Emily Jane. As we sat in the steaming water the aches and cares of the long season seemed to fade away. Then we heard an odd noise and looked out into the inlet - it was a humpback whale blowing as it surfaced: a totally magic experience!

Right: looking down from the top of the penstock at Butedale Cannery, *Mile 473.* The water flowing through the penstock turned the generators that powered the cannery and the little town surrounding it. Sadly, it is now mostly abandoned.

A - Routes divide: whenever possible small craft seek the narrower channels providing the most shelter. In the Desolation Sound - Discovery Islands area, this winding route offers more protection and places to anchor, tie up for the night, etc. than the big ship route further west via Seymour Narrows.

B - Johnstone Straits: this is sort of the Route 1 of the Inside Passage; all craft small and large must use it. It is essentially a wide and windy canyon, especially in the summer when interior British Columbia heats up, drawing cooler heavier air through Johnstone Strait, creating the infamous westerlies.

C - Routes divide - small craft travel cautiously here, often laying at **Gods Pocket, Mile 310**, setting the alarm for 3 a.m., sniffing the weather and if it looks good, heading across to sheltered Fitzhugh Sound.

D - The Northern Canyons is my nickname for this part of the traditional Inside Passage that winds through the mountain heart of British Columbia. When cruise ships were smaller, they all took this very scenic route, but sadly today most take the wider and much more boring route straight up **Hecate Strait**.

E - Occasionally in good settled weather, Juneau bound ships will travel further west up and along the outside coast of **Haida Gwaii,** previously known as the Queen Charlotte Islands. This is a particularly remote and rugged coast.

F - When a big tide is flooding against a southerly gale, the entire north end of Hecate Strait can be covered with dangerous breakers.

Rivers Inlet, east of **Mile 325** *was busy in the 1910s, 20s, and 30s summers with hundreds of small gillnetters, and five canneries, even a small hotel. Sadly, the runs were overfished and the river valleys heavily logged. Today the canneries are slowly disappearing into the forest except for Goose Bay, which has been repurposed as a sports fishing lodge.*

Top: blackfish (local word for killer whales or orcas) at Rivers Inlet, circa 1910. Boats are engineless salmon gillnetters. At the beginning of each five day fishing period, a tug would tow all the gillnetters out into the vastness of the nearby inlets. Each day a fish buyer would make the rounds of the boats, and at the end of the period, the tug would tow everyone back to the cannery! BCARS B-04100

*Mile 600 - Alaska Canada border. A lonely, windy place; most boats hurry across. No duty free shopping. 15 miles east is **Tongass Island**, where native villagers were outraged to get back from a 1920 hunting trip and discover that one of their totems had been stolen by a passing boat. They chased the boat by canoe, but were unable to catch up. The totem ended up in Seattle's Pioneer Square.*

When that one rotted away, Seattle town fathers contacted the tribe they had stolen it from to carve another. Wisely, the tribe demanded payment in advance, and when they received it, said that it paid for the totem that had been stolen 50 years earlier! So Seattle had to cough up twice to get the new totem!

Want to see whales? Just keep your binoculars with you. Whales, particularly humpbacks, are seen all along the Northwest coast. And they're easy to find.

Whales are mammals, meaning they need to breathe on the surface. When they do, they exhale dramatically, creating a spout of water mixed with air that can be seen for miles, as in "Thar she blows."

Typically, whales will linger on the surface, breathing slowly, usually making shallow short dives between breaths. Then, when they lift their tail like the whale is doing in the picture to the right, it means that the whale will be "sounding," or diving deep, and may be down for as long as 15 minutes before coming up the surface again.

If you are lucky, you'll see a breach like the bottom photo in which a humpback jumps clear of the water and lands with a terrific splash that may be seen for miles. It's not clear why they do this. Perhaps they are dislodging parasites.

You also may see bubble-feeding, when a group of humpbacks will circle a school of herring, breathing to create a fence of bubbles, then surface dramatically through the school with their mouths open.

Orcas, or "killer" whales, are the other commonly seen whale. These are smaller, up to 30 feet, but are easily recognized by their tall scimitar-like dorsal fins. They are aggressive feeders, chowing down on salmon, seals, sea lions, and sometimes even smaller whales.

Both orcas and humpbacks can be seen throughout the range that Alaska cruise ships travel.

Top: School of orcas in Johnstone Strait, B.C. Their tall dorsal fins and black and white markings make them easy to identify. Minden Pictures

Middle: A humpback lifts his tail before diving, as seen on a Juneau whale-watching tour.

*Bottom: A dramatic humpback breach in Frederick Sound, Alaska, near **Mile 845**, photographed by commercial fisherman Duncan Kowalski.*

NAVIGATION IN THE IPAD ERA

It used to be when you went north with a boat, you'd have to bring a stack of charts, or at the least two or three heavy spiral-bound chartbooks, plus two tide books (Canada and US), plus dividers, parallel rulers, and Coast Pilots (textbook-like guidebooks). And, you'd need space for all this plus space to unfold the big charts. This was all very challenging on a typical small boat.

Today that is so Old School. That heavy stack of charts has in most vessels been replaced by a chart-plotter, a device that receives a GPS signal from satellites and displays your position in real time as an icon on a moving chart. In recent, years, Apps for the iPad, iPhone, and other devices do the same thing.

Recently I took a 10-day trip with friends to the islands that straddle the Canada–Washington border. The App on my iPhone, which cost $10, was more accurate than the dedicated GPS plotter on board.

The GPS on the iPhone is from Navionics, available at the App Store. It's a great way to follow your route and compare it with the maps in this book.

Top: Lopez Pass, San Juan Islands, is seen on a paper chart with dividers for measuring distance and parallel rulers for determining a boat's course.

Right: Screens of the same area on iPad (top) and iPhone (bottom). The little triangle on the iPad screen shows the position of the user's boat.

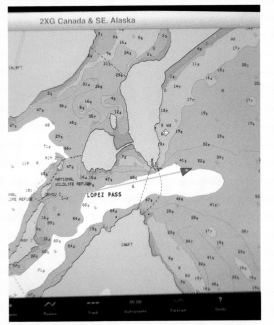

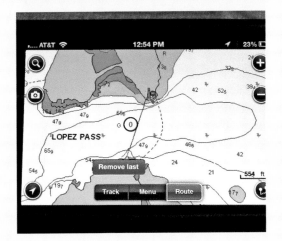

Mile 607 - *Tree Point Lighthouse*, *also look for salmon gilletters, like the above, working these waters. If you see much larger vessels they are probably tenders or fish buying vessels.*

Mile 610

Mile 625 - *Boca de Quadra - the largest molybdenum open pit mine in the world was planned for the spectacular wilderness here before the cold war ended and with it the demand for so much moly. (Used in jet engines.)*

Mile 630- *Annette Island to the west is the home of the Tsimshian tribe of Alaska natives.*

The first salmon cannery in Alaska was built in 1887 and shortly thereafter many different operators came and built canneries wherever there was a protected harbor and a good salmon run. As many were in remote areas, the early canneries were whole little self contained towns.

But the advent of refrigerated transport vessels, or tenders, allowed the canneries to move into existing towns where operating costs were lower.

Below: the old Sunny Point cannery, Ketchikan.

The coast of Southeast Alaska, like British Columbia, is deeply indented with inlets winding far back into the mountainous and forbidding interior. The islands, large and small, form a maze of channels. In the northern part, glaciers lie at the head of many of the inlets, discharging ice year round.

Most of the area is thickly forested, without settlements or towns, little changed since the arrival of the white man. Almost all the land is owned by federal and state governments; little is available for sale to individuals.

There are a few towns. Each has a few miles of roads, few are connected to each other or to the "outside." Most travel is by boat or plane.

Scattered in little coves and harbors far from the towns are a few roadless communities that still enjoy a quiet existence. Except for storekeepers and the fish-buyers, residents mostly fish for salmon. In summer, they scatter up and down the coast, hustling to make a year's pay in a few months.

Then comes the fall. The outside boats straggle back to Washington State harbors, the days get shorter, and the sun disappears behind thick clouds. Weeks pass with only an occasional boat or float plane arriving to break the monotony.

Despite short days and gloomy weather, many local residents prefer winter. After the rush of the salmon season, winter can be a welcome change with time to work on cabin or boat, visit with neighbors, or just sit and read. It's not a fast-paced life, but there's enough to do. Many residents have spent time in the larger towns and wouldn't think of moving back.

Top: ice from Le Conte Glacier east of Petersburg, sometimes drifts into upper Frederick Sound, creating a hazard to mariners. DK photo
Above: on the docks at Wrangell.

SOUTHEAST ALASKA
Points of Interest:

1. Glacier Bay: In 1794, English explorer George Vancouver, found no bay, just solid ice all the way out to Icy Strait.

2. Lynn Canal: Surrounded by high mountains and glaciers, this waterway can be a fierce wind tunnel.

3. Admiralty Island National Monument: This area is essentially all wilderness except for the native village of Angoon. It is home to a large population of brown bears.

4. Tracy and Endicott arms: These arms lead back to glaciers, often visited by cruise ships.

5. Frederick Sound and Stephens Passage: humpbacks usually sighted here, also small icebergs are occasionally seen in this area .

6. Chatham Strait: ruins of old canneries and whale, herring, and codfish plants are still found in many of the bays here. Salmon runs remain strong but refrigerated transport vessels take the fish to towns such as Petersburg for processing.

7. Point Baker: With its population of about 35, Point Baker is one of many roadless communities scattered throughout this island archipelago. Most residents are commercial fishers. Your mapmaker built a cabin here and wrote about his many adventures in his memoir, Alaska Blues.

8. Le Conte Bay: This is the most southerly place that a glacier reaches down to the saltwater. Off the beaten path, the rapidly retreating glacier calves its icebergs into a particularly beautiful bay.

9. Petersburg: Settled by Norwegian fishermen, today this town is the commercial fishing center of SE Alaska and has a bustling waterfront lined with canneries and fish freezer plants.

10. Wrangell Narrows: a winding, 22-mile shortcut between Ketchikan and Juneau, widely used by small craft and Alaska state ferries. It is too narrow for big ships.

11. The Border Peaks: the U.S.-Canada border runs along the top of the highest peaks of the coastal range.

12. Stikine River: winds though the coastal mountains. Early gold-rush route to interior.

13. Prince of Wales Island: This is the fourth-largest island in the U.S. (after Kodiak, Hawaii, and Puerto Rico). During the heyday of logging in the 1960s, it was one of the wealthiest of Alaska zip codes. (Loggers are well paid.)

14. The Outside coast: There is only one town, Sitka, found on this very rough and remote 400-mile stretch of coast, seen in the map to right. Any lights you may see at night are apt to be anchored fishing boats.

15. Misty Fjords National Monument: This very rugged high country is penetrated by several deep and winding fjords. Excursions are available from Ketchikan to Rudyard Bay, a dramatic fjord.

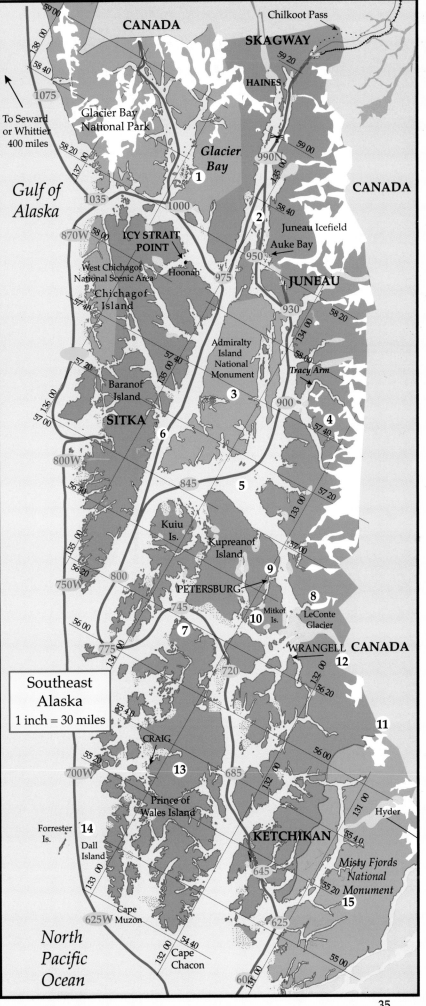

Exploring:
Ketchikan

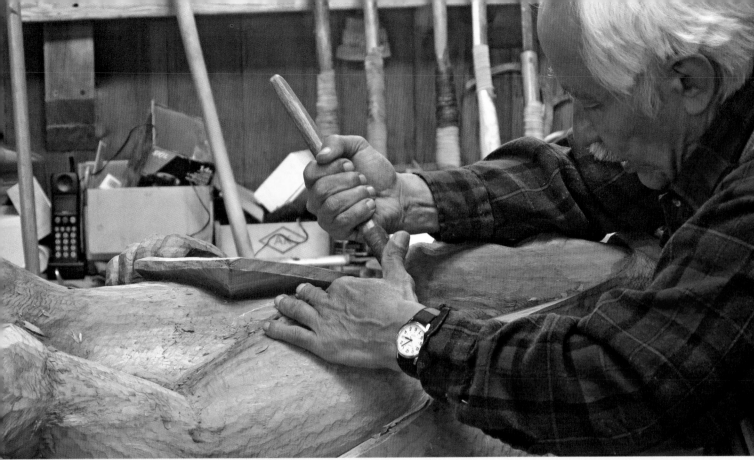

Twenty miles long and two blocks wide isn't a bad way to describe Ketchikan, originally a rough–and-tumble fishing town, where Creek Street, the red-light district, was a busy place, especially on the weekends when both fishermen and loggers came in to kick up their heels.

The U.S. Forest Service facilitated the big Ketchikan Pulp Mill in the early 1950s, and a sawmill operated on the docks where cruise ships tie up today. It was a welcome change from the earlier days when most jobs existed only during the salmon season, and everyone lived on credit during the long winters. In pulp mill days, logging was king, and many commercial fishermen felt like second-class citizens.

Unfortunately, careless logging practices reduced salmon catches and angered commercial fishermen. Tougher logging regulations came, and the mill closed in 1997.

Fortunately, commercial fishing is strong again. The cruise industry has created many seasonal jobs. Yet, without a large-year round employer like the old pulp mill, the 8,000 or so residents of Ketchikan still find that winter can be a lean and slow time economically after the big cruise ships stop coming.

Have a look at the fishing boats in Thomas Basin, just south of downtown. Once they leave town, many boats are out for a week or more at a time. Years ago, most salmon was canned, but today a large portion gets frozen or air freighted out fresh to lower 48 markets.

A good walk is south of town - turn right off your ship - about two miles, past canneries and the Coast Guard Station, to **Saxman Village,** an authentic native community with carving shed, dancers, and numerous totems. A city bus also stops right in front; info/schedule at village office.

Opposite top: waterfront statue celebrating town history. Opposite lower right: loggers at the logging show downtown.

Lower left: Creek Street, just a short walk from downtown is the old red light district. As they used to say, "Where the fishermen and the fish came to spawn." Don't miss artist Ray Troll's gallery - his t-shirt art is a staple of Northwest culture!

This page top: Nathan Jackson carving a new totem pole at the Saxman carving shed. Totems are made of rot resistant cedar, but still they will only last 68-80 years sitting out in the rain all the time. Left: Tlingit girl and totem, circa 1930.

Flightseeing the Boca and other excursions

(Subject to change)
Misty Fjords—by air or sea, or a combination
Bering Sea Fishermen's Tour on a crab boat
Coastal Wildlife Cruise
Wilderness Exploration and Crab Feast
Sea Kayaking
Rainforest Wildlife Sanctuary Hike
Neets Bay Bear Watch and Seaplane Flight
Rainforest Ropes Course and Zipline Park
Bear Creek Zipline
Adventure Kart Expedition
Back Country Hummer Expedition—U Drive
Flightseeing and Crab Feast
Totem Bight Park and Town Tour
Totem Bight and Lumberjack Show Combo
Saxman Native Village Tour
Town and Harbor Duck Tour
Motorcycle Tour—U Drive
Sports-fishing Expedition
Sports-fishing & Wilderness Dining
Alaskan Chef's Table
City Highlights Trolley Tour
Mountain Point Snorkeling Adventure
And, as they say, many more...

Note: sometimes if excursions are sold out at a ship's excursion office, they still may be available for purchase right on the dock.

Top: Flight-seeing plane entering Misty Fjords. Tours by fast boat are also available.

Left, middle: The Aleutian Ballad takes visitors to nearby waters to experience what life is like aboard a "Deadliest Catch" style king crab boat.

Left, bottom: totem poles and lodge at Saxman Village.

BEAR COUNTRY

When the salmon run in Alaska, first they travel up streams to their spawning grounds, then after the female lays and the male fertilizes the eggs, both fish die. Their remains comprise a major part of the yearly diet of both black and brown bears and eagles.

The largest population of bears in SE Alaska are black, up to perhaps 600 pounds. Most brown or grizzly bears live in western Alaska, though there are populations on Admiralty Island and in scattered coastal locations. "Brownies" are huge. The males weight as much as a ton!

Top and lower left: Bears at Anan Creek north of Ketchikan. Don't think you can escape a bear by climbing a tree.

Left-middle and above: Brown bears (identified by the hump on their shoulders) in the Brooks Falls area of the Katmai National Park west of Anchorage. This was a too-close encounter for our son and I!

THE NOME NUGGET

NOME, ALASKA, SATURDAY, JANUARY...

DIPHTHERIA EPIDEMIC THREATENS

MAYOR APPOINTS PUBLIC HEALTH NURSE FOR EPIDEMIC.

NOME QUARANTINE CITY. MAYOR MAYNARD CLOSES SCHOOLS; REQESTS ALL TRAFFIC IN AND OUT OF NOME TO STOP. VILLAGES ALLERTED VIA WIRELESS MESSAGE OF DIPHTHERIA EPIDEMIC.

ANTITOXIN IN NOME IS OLD; DR WELLS SAID FIVE YEAR ANTITOXIN IS NOT ENOUGH TO DO THE JOB.

DEATH RACE BEGINS

ALASKA RAILROADS STEAM ENGINE 66 WITH CHARLIE MATHIESON, ENGINEER, BEGAN 298 MILE RUN TO NENANA WITH ANTITOXIN FOR NOME; WILD BILL SHANNON WITH DOG TEAM WAITS IN -30° TEMPERATURE IN NENANA

DOG TEAM STARTED STRICKEN NOME ANTITOXIN

NENANA, JAN 28 WILD BILL SHANNON STRING OF EIGHT... TOLOVANA, TEM... THE DOG TRAIL... BELOW ZERO. THE SERUM IS... AND CANVAS... FREEZING D...

30,000 B.C.: Migratory hunters from Asia move across the land bridge from Siberia to Alaska, and settle North America.

8,000 B.C.: As the Ice Age ends, the rising ocean covers the land bridge. An ice bridge forms. Migration slows.

1741: Vitus Bering and Aleksei Chirikov land in Alaska on an expedition from Russia and take home 800 sea otter skins, but Bering is lost on the return. The fur traders begin outfitting new expeditions, and the fur rush is on.

1778: British Captain James Cook explores much of the Alaskan coast.

1792-4: British Captain George Vancouver exhaustively explores and charts the Northwest Coast with two ships.

1799: Alexander Baranov consolidates Russia's possession of Alaska with establishment of a fort and trading base at Sitka.

1867: Secretary of State William Seward buys Alaska from Russia for 2 cents an acre. Total purchase price: $7.2 million. By then, however, the fur resource has been depleted. The land deal is hailed as "Seward's Folly."

1879: Naturalist John Muir canoes throughout SE Alaska and discovers Glacier Bay. (When Captain Vancouver passed through, there was no bay to be seen, just ice.) Muir's reports inspire development of early tourism industry.

1896-1900: A gold strike on a Yukon River tributary attracts 100,000 people to the Yukon Territory and Alaska.

1922: Roy Jones makes the first floatplane flight up the Inside Passage. It revolutionized bush travel in Alaska.

1925: A 674-mile dog sled relay brings diphtheria vaccine to Nome. The feat is celebrated today with the annual running of the Iditarod Trail Sled Dog Race from Anchorage to Nome.

1942: Japan invades the Aleutian Islands. The Alaska Highway project is begun to move defense supplies into the territory.

1959: Alaska becomes the 49th state.

1964: Good Friday earthquake kills 131 people in Alaska. It's a giant, the second-worst earthquake ever recorded.

1968: Ten billion barrels of oil are discovered at Prudhoe Bay.

1971: Congress settles Alaska Native land claims, conveying 40 million acres of land and $1 billion to the state's Natives.

1976: Federal 200-mile limit established around all US coastline, sets stage for major fisheries growth in Alaska .

1977: The first oil flows through the 800-mile trans-Alaska pipeline, a monumental engineering feat.

1980: Congress passes the Alaska National Interest Lands and Conservation Act (ANILCA), establishing millions of acres of Federal park lands, wilderness areas, refuges, and other park units.

1989: The tanker *Exxon Valdez* rams a reef creating a massive oil spill and years of work for hundreds of lawyers.

2011 - US Supreme Court finally settles punitive damages to be paid by Exxon for spill, reducing award by 75%.

Opposite top; ivory walrus tusk in Dennis Corrington's Skagway Museum celebrates the famous effort to get the diphtheria vaccine to Nome via dogsled in bitter minus 30 degree weather.

Opposite right middle: an Aleut native gets ready to harpoon a sea otter. Otters, valued in Asia for their very thick pelt, created Alaska's first resource boom, beginning in the 1740s. The Russians treated the natives brutally, threating to destroy whole villages if the villagers didn't bring in enough pelts. UW NA1995

Opposite right lower: the next big boom was salmon, which still is a very important part of the Alaska economy. Before statehood in 1959, most salmon were caught by fish traps, owned by Seattle fishing companies. Fish traps were banned as part of Alaska's becoming the 49th state. Tongass Historical

Opposite left middle: one of many gold dredges that worked Alaska's rivers in the early to mid 1900s. These dig up the river bottoms and process it to extract any gold. UW 1796D

Opposite left bottom: visitors at an Alaska pipeline viewing area near Fairbanks. The odd looking finned structures on top are passive radiators, designed to cool the pipeline's foundations so that the permafrost below the surface doesn't melt and allow the pipeline to sink.

Right: look at these faces aboard a Yukon River paddle wheel steamer during the 1898 - 99 Klondike Gold Rush. UW Thwaites 0394-1286.

THE FIRST PEOPLE: AN ENDURING CULTURE

Wandering over the land bridge from Asia during the last ice age, spreading out among the islands of what is now Southeast Alaska, the First People learned that the sea and the forest provided. Eventually becoming primarily in Southeast Alaska the Tlingit, Haida, and Tsimshian, they endured the brutality of the Russians and new diseases to which they had no immunity, creating stable communities with time to create substantial art.

When the Russians sold Alaska to the US in 1867, both the seller and buyer seemed to have ignored the fact that a good deal of the vast region already belonged to the Natives.

The issue of Native land claims had to be settled before the Alaska oil pipeline could be built in the 1970s. Part of the $1 billion, 40-million-acre settlement created regional Native corporations, each of which received a substantial amount of money from the Federal government. The new corporations invested in many things, including the Mount Roberts Tram in Juneau.

Yet, even after the settlement, much of the income in the Native villages of SE Alaska still comes from fishing and logging.

Photographs on these two pages were taken at Celebration 2010, the biannual Natives arts and culture festival held in Juneau. Natives from all around SE Alaska come to the capital to celebrate their heritage. The parade is a not-to-be-missed event.

Fortunately, unlike British Columbia, Alaska's fishery resources have been well managed and are generally strong. Refrigerated fish-transport vessels, called tenders or packers, bring in fish from remote areas to processing in the towns.

Commercial fishing is tightly regulated by area, gear type, and fishing time. The return of salmon to streams is carefully monitored and fishing time tailored to make sure enough salmon return to spawn to create the next generation.

In recent years, processors have moved to build facilities to freeze more of their salmon instead of canning it, creating a higher-value product. Salmon roe, for export to Japan, has evolved to be a premium product.

Many young men and women who put themselves through college by working on Alaska fishing boats have discovered that such work makes for a great job after college as well. In the recent big years, many of the crews on good purse seiners, such as the one on the opposite page, made close to $50,000 for the three-month season while crew shares on top boats might double that!

Top: a herring skiff during the Kah Shakes Cove roe herring fishery.

Left: Your author's crew unloads at the tender, Naknek River, Bristol Bay, western Alaska. A cannery is just a half mile away, so the fish are processed quickly without needing to be refrigerated.

Top: a salmon purse seiner, which encircles schools of fish with its net, pulls the bunt, or end of the net, aboard. DK photo.

Above: valuable salmon eggs being sorted in a Petersburg cannery. The cannery boss told me jokingly that eggs were getting so valuable he was thinking of getting a guard to ride shotgun on the forklift.

Right: Many of the smaller gillnet or trolling vessels are operated by couples, or occasionally just one person.

ALONG THE WAY: KETCHIKAN TO JUNEAU

"Ratz Harbor, Mile 695, Oct. 26, 1974 - Lured out this afternoon by a break in the weather, after two days of laying here with violent winds battering us. Big mistake - wind came up again at Narrow Pt, 2 mi. south, stirred up big tide rip; lucky to get back in here without breaking windows out. Traded booze for frozen pork chops and instant spuds at logging camp.

Mile 695

Mile 685 - Meyers Chuck, *pop. 21, one of numerous roadless fishing communities, allowing very small craft to fish close to home.*

Top: Breaching humpback, near **Mile 670.** *It's not clear why whales do this—perhaps to dislodge parasites? But breaching is spectacular, and fairly common—keep your eyes peeled.* Alaskastock

Above: though 'Inside', these waters can be challenging for small craft. This is the Cape Hason, *with whom we were traveling when we encountered the tide rip in the journal entry on the left.*

Right: Sea lions at a rookery near Tracy Arm. The big guy is a bull, who might weigh a ton or more. He would often live with a "harem" and guard them jealously. When we approached in our inflatable boat, he jumped in, swam over, and threatened us with his sharp teeth. Being in a boat with just a thin rubber and nylon hull, we got the message!

Northern Clarence Straits, Mile 690 to Mile 730, *is a salmon gillnet area. Boats are typically 35-45 feet long and usually operated by one or two people, often a couple. Most boats ice down their fish in their holds and deliver at the end of the Sun-Wed fishing period to fish processors in either Wrangell or Petersburg.*

The gillnets used here are about 1200' long by 25' deep. Made of thin nylon dyed to match the color of the water, they are stored on a big drum in the stern. To fish, they are rolled off the drum and hang like a shallow fence in the water, catching little else except salmon.

Top: big barge in Wrangell Narrows, north of **Mile 730.** *This one is probably loaded with canned and frozen salmon from Bristol Bay, about 1000 miles further west and north. A weekly barge serves Ketchikan, Sitka, Juneau, Haines, and Skagway, bringing up about everything you can imagine from Seattle. Note the vehicle on top.*

Above: big iceberg, near the mouth of Le Conte Bay, Frederick Sound, southeast of **Mile 870.** *Luckily few bergs this big drift into the main cruise ship lanes in Stevens Passage.*

Left: old crank victrola in an abandoned house on **Harbor Island, Mile 900.**

Mile 720 - Snow Passage - constricted channel creates current swirls that often bring herring to surface, attracting whales. Also look for a big sea lion that often hangs out on the big red buoy on the east side of the channel.

Mile 730

Mile 730 - routes split; smaller vessels, including the 420' Alaska State ferry Columbia *travel north via twisting and constricted* **Wrangell Narrows.** *Large cruise ships continue west into Sumner Strait.*

The ironic thing about almost all that gorgeous waterfront land that you are passing is that almost all of it belongs to Alaska and Federal governments; almost none is for sale except right around the towns.

But for entrepreneurial families, there was an alternative: build a floating home on a raft made up of logs hauled off the beaches. These guys did just that - living in the tiny cabin on the left while they build a larger one with wood from their portable sawmill. Of course, life in a floating home has its own little wrinkles - when the little cabin on the left got too small for the two busy little boys, Mom sent them out to fish - in the outhouse!

HOW STORMY GOT HIS NAME

My wife and I operated a fish buying vessel in 1982, and became friends with the Hamars, who fished for us. Their oldest son was named Stormy. I asked how he got his name. His mother Ethel:

"We were beachlogging Ratz Harbor when I was pregnant - hauling big logs off the beach to sell to the pulp mill. We were living on our little fishboat; that was going to be our winter money. I went into labor just as we had the logs all rafted up, and ready to get towed over to the mill. We called a plane, but George had to stay meet the tug that was coming for the logs. He said he'd ride over with the tug to Ketchikan and meet me in the hospital.

"It was so stormy that it took the floatplane three passes before it could even land. But finally we got over to Ketchikan and I went right in to the hospital and had a healthy little boy. But it was a wild night; the wind was just howling and the rain slashing at the windows.

"George came in the next morning. Right off I could tell that something bad had happened; his face was all downcast.

"What is it?" I asked, "What happened?"

"We lost them logs. The raft busted up coming across Clarence Strait. They're all scattered now; we'll never get paid."

I put our firstborn into his arms, and his expression lifted.

"What should we call him?" He asked.

"How about Stormy?" I said, "For the night he was born.."

THE FLOATING LODGES

Fishing lodges and aquaculture facilities also found it convenient to be floating. First if you built on the land, you had to either own the land - none too easy - (Coastal land for sale in Alaska is hard to find) - or you had to get all the permits to operate on US Forest Service land, (also not so easy) and get monitored regularly. Plus.. fish move; what may be a hot spot one year may be a dead zone the next. With lodges you can basically set up where the fish are. And as you are basically a boat, you can anchor where you want with fewer restrictions. Some lodges are moored permanently with their own floating breakwaters, and others are towed back to town in the winter for easier maintenance.

Top: floating fishing lodge near Esperanza Inlet, on the west coast of Vancouver Island. This was in late September, the salmon season was over and the lodge will soon be in the caretaker's hands.

*Left upper: once I was steaming up Grenville Channel in upper British Columbia and looked out at this amazing sight: a three- and a four-story lodge, complete with decks and plenty of Victorian trim, both built on barges and on their way to the Hakai Pass fishing grounds, west of **Mile 375** where they would be anchored for the season!*

Lower left: this bunkhouse/warehouse, tucked into a tiny and steep sided cove, is near a salmon farm in Machalat Inlet, B.C.

Mile 745 - Point Baker and its close neighbor **Port Protection** *are popular stopping places for traveling mariners. In the 70s and 80s, it featured a floating bar/general store, whose owner was also the fish buyer. (You could sell your catch for bar credit). When it got crowded on a Saturday night you better be wearing boots, as water would start to seep up through the floor!*

*Mile 748 - winding away to the north between Kuiu and Kupreanof Islands is Keku Strait, known to locals as **Rocky Pass**. Before GPS it was a 'local knowledge only' sort of place, but now many small craft use it each summer.*

Exploring:
Baird Glacier

The US- Canada border runs through the rugged mountains of the coastal range north and east of Baird Glacier. Two notable peaks, popular with climbers are the **Devil's Thumb, 9,077'**, and **Kate's Needle, 10,002'**.

Icebergs from **Le Conte Glacier** sometimes drift right into the harbor in Petersburg, and early fishermen used the icebergs to chill the fish they took down to Seattle in the days before refrigeration.

In August, 2014, we stopped in here aboard the small ship, *Wilderness Adventurer*. As you can see, receding glaciers change substantially as they melt. We were fortunate; after we climbed the 60' terminal moraine, we found that the melt water pool that had blocked hikers the year before, had drained away, allowing us to actually climb up and walk around the austere moonscape that was the top of the glacier.

Helped by a harbor too small for the big ships, Petersburg town fathers decided to just do what they do best: catch and process fish. Settled by Norwegian immigrants, who'd fished in the old country, they felt right at home here with the dramatic mountains and strong fishery resources.

Just north of cannery row, modest houses lined the street overlooking Wrangell Narrows and Frederick Sound. From their living rooms and dining tables, the families could look out at the boats headed home from the fishing grounds. After work the men could stroll home along the water. Not a bad life.

Ole Sjonning Husvik
1890 – 1961
"Ya, vi ha it god in America"

LIFE IN A ROADLESS COMMUNITY

It was the swiftly running tide near Mile 745 that caused Captain Johnny O'Brien's luck to run out in the black of a November night in 1917. His Mariposa was one of the finest steamers on the Alaska run, but while Johnny slept and the pilot steered, the current set her off course and onto Mariposa Reef, where pieces of her still remain.

Mile 742 ▷

Mile 745 ▷

Hole in the Wall, east of Mile 751, is one of Alaska's special places. A channel so narrow that trollers must use care if their poles are down leads to a tranquil and lake-like basin where deer and bear may be seen along the shore.

Tucked into two coves south of **Mile 746** are two communities about three miles apart, each with about 60 folks. The summer salmon season is a busy time, with folks trying to make a full year's pay in just a few short months. Some fish in the nearby Sumner Strait gillnet area, others move aboard their boats for the season, following the fish up and down the coast.

In the 1970s, a person could lease a piece of waterfront land from The US Forest Service for a few thousand dollars a year, build a cabin with timber from the local forest, and make enough money in a boat as small as an open skiff, to get by on: pretty sweet!

These days the emphasis is more on hosting sports fishermen who stay at one of three lodges, but there still is a floating bar!

AT THE POINT BAKER FLOATING BAR

Of course, a floating bar where the bartender is also the fish buyer in town, and where you can sell your fish for bar credit, is apt to be a colorful place.

For example, once a couple arrived in a small yacht, obviously not commercial fishermen as were most of the clientele of the bar.

The bartender came over, laid a big thick arm on the bar: "What'll it be?"

"How about a Manhatten?" Said the gal.

"I'll take a whiskey sour." Said the man.

"Look," said the bartender, "we have whiskey and water, whiskey and Coke, whiskey and Tang. And we save ice for the fish."

My neighbor, Flea, around 1973. He had a little cabin on the water, his Social Security, fished every day, and grabbed a beer from the fish buyer for the run back home: not a bad retirement!

The Point Baker floating Post Office in the 1970s. In those days the mailboat stopped around midnight on Wednesday. So on Thursday all sorts of characters would appear to pick up their mail, likely containing their weed for the week as well!

BUILDING A HOME IN THE NORTH

We found a nearby island, on a private cove, with a gorgeous western exposure and view, for $17,000. After the season, in our houseboat on Seattle's Lake Union, we made plans for a cabin. As our money dwindled, so did the size of our new-home-to-be until whatever roof we could get over our heads for fifteen hundred bucks would have to be it. We settled on a 12-by-16-foot box with a half loft, 275-square-feet, total: tiny.

We scoured garage sales and second-hand stores, found a big diesel oil range for $35, all our windows and doors for $175. I built a kitchen counter, complete with sink and drawers. We purchased a 16-foot cedar skiff with a 10-horsepower, 1958 Evinrude outboard. Tool by tool, fitting by fitting, we packed the supplies aboard my 32-foot gill-net vessel and skiff to tow north.

Shortly after arriving in Point Baker, the mail boat arrived with our large bundle of lumber. The plan had been to tow the tightly strapped bundle through the channel to our secluded cove and house site. But it was so green and dense, it wouldn't even float. It was what the locals called, "pond dried." So we put it temporarily on the dock and then hauled it in our skiff, load by load out the channel to our site.

We struggled to get the cabin up: the wood was so wet it splashed when your hammer missed the nail. It rained; every night we would take the skiff back to our boat at the Point Baker dock, heat up something quick, and fall, exhausted, shivering, into our sleeping bags.

And created something exquisite: out every window was the water. As we ate at the driftwood table, we could see eagles swooping, curious seals, and most marvelous of all, a pair of humpbacks that hung out in the tide rips by West Rock, off the mouth of our cove. On still nights, we could hear the sigh-like breathing of the whales as they surfaced and exchanged fresh air for stale.

We called our little cove Port Upton. We dragged huge logs off the beach, got more lumber from town to build a big float to work on our nets. Just us and our friends in that wild and remote cove.

When the first snow came one November evening, the fire in the wood stove crackled cheerily and our kerosene lamp shone out on the vast and wild world beyond the windows.

It was magic.

Exploring:
Lonely Chatham Strait

Cape Decision Light-house, Mile 775, is a major turning point, and the entrance to Chatham Strait. It is at the very southern tip of Kuiu Island, about the size of Maui, but with just 10 inhabitants.

Mile 870

Port Alexander, Mile 895 is the only settlement in lower Chatham Strait. In the 1920s and 30s, with strong salmon runs, it was a money-kissed little place, where a resident once told a new arrival that it was illegal to walk the streets sober. Then the great dams on the Columbia River were built, cutting off the fish from their spawning grounds, and within a decade or so, the population of Port Alexander shrank from 2,500 to a hundred or less.

Chatham Strait stretches for almost 150 miles, deep, wide, and today, for the most part empty and lonely. But poke into almost any bay and you'll find evidence of a much more prosperous past. Whales, codfish, herring, and of course salmon were caught here. Whales were rendered into oil, herring into oil and fishmeal, and salmon were salted and also canned. The whaling stations, salteries, and canneries were all in remote bays, close to the resource, but distant from the nearest large town, Juneau or Petersburg. The result was that each processing plant essentially had to be a whole little town unto itself with mess halls, bunkhouses for workers, houses for management, warehouses, generators, etc.

At the head of **Big Port Walter, Mile 800**, are the buildings of the old Alaska Pacific Herring Co. now slowly falling into the bay. In the herring boom days of the 30s, 40s, and 50s, big seiners took load after load of herring here. It was also the wettest place in North America, with an average of almost 250 inches a year. What must it have been like there for the caretaker and his family, when the sun disappeared over the high mountains for months at time, and the bay froze over solid?

A few miles south is **Port Conclusion**, where Captain Vancouver and his two ships lay anchored in August, 1794, waiting for his smaller boats filling in the last blank places on his chart of Southeast Alaska. Finally on the 19th they showed up. So with grog for all hands and cheers ringing from ship to ship so far from England, there ended one of the most remarkable feats of exploration in modern times. In three long seasons of charting this unknown (to whites..) coast, through persistent fogs, strong currents, even icebergs, Vancouver had disproved the ages-old notion of a Northwest Passage through the continent back to the Atlantic.

I saw the Strait first when I was 19, working on an Alaska fishboat. I'd get the night watches, down Chatham. I'd turn down the radar and instruments until I could just make out the dim loom of the high land on either side of the strait. All that shore, all that land, but never a light or a boat; for a kid, raised on the urban East Coast, it was stunning.

Top: the Cape Decision Lighthouse with Cape Ommaney, on the other side of Chatham Strait in the distance.

Right: a Port Alexander resident talks about the old days. When I stopped in there in my fish buying boat in 1975, everyone had their own home brew for us to try!

54

Tebenkof Bay, Mile 805, was a popular spot for very small commercial salmon trollers or hand-trollers, with its protected arms and a fish buyer also selling fuel and groceries.

Bay of Pillars, Mile 815, was the site of yet another cannery, now just pilings on the beach and some rusty tanks and boilers. At the head of the bay a big anchored tug, the Sea Ranger, serves as a base lodge for fly-in sports fishing groups.

A veteran's organization, Bay of Pillars, Inc. has built a lodge on the site of the old cannery to provide wilderness experiences for veterans and their families.

Baranof Hot Springs, Mile 855CS, with a lodge and a dozen or so seasonal houses is a pretty popular spot on summer weekends with the fishing fleet is in town. A long soak and beer and baked salmon on the dock with your fishing buddies is a great way to relax after a hard week of fishing.

Top: loaded deep with herring, the American Star approaches the dock at Big Port Walter. The way into the bay is a narrow cut through the head of what at first seems like a dead end channel. Yet the big Standard Oil tanker even made regular stops back when the herring plant was in operation.

Above: a big sperm whale hauled out on the slipway at Port Armstrong, Mile 790, around 1930. Today the shore of the bay is home to a salmon hatchery. Of course all the fish also attract bears. which has proved to be a real challenge for the hatchery operators. Over the years they have tried electric fences, firecrackers, even a giant potato gun in efforts to deter the bears without harming them.
Mohai 15329

Left: hand troller. Towing just two lines (with numerous baits and lures) with hand cranked winches is a low cost way to enter the fishery.

Exploring:
Le Conte Bay

Around 7/8's of an ice-berg's mass is underwater and melts at a much faster rate than the top, just exposed to the air. As this part melts, the center of gravity changes, and a berg can topple without warning.

Mile 1010

Top: Le Conte bergs with Horn Cliff, across Frederick Sound from Petersburg in the background.

Right: Filmmaker Dan - this is actually a bit dangerous, as we discovered that grounded bergs like this one can collapse or fall over without any warning.

Off the beaten path, hidden in the coastal mountains east of Petersburg, is Le Conte Bay. It's a stunning spot—one of Alaska's secret places—but with unpredictable, rapidly changing weather and swiftly flowing tides. The bay presented challenging conditions for filmmaker Dan Kowalski and me.

But we found a place on the beach to set up video cameras and audio recorder. At the edge of the place where we were filming was a small beached iceberg, about the size of a dump truck. I was thinking of going over and leaning against it. Before I could do it, the iceberg suddenly collapsed with big chunks crashing onto the very place I would have been standing.

I was lucky that day. It was a reminder that the wilderness is always waiting—for the foolish, for the careless, and or just the unlucky.

In the early evening, after the tide eased, we anchored away from the ice, and climbed into the skiff to go out among the big bergs.

We let the sun get a little lower, find some clouds to diffuse it, and suddenly we had that moment with the perfect soft light that filmmakers wait for.

We turned the motor off, and I let the currents push us in a slow circle among the bergs while I talked and Dan filmed. It was perfect.

We shot until dusk, then it was time to pick our way through the bergs in the failing light and get across lower Frederick Sound to a safe anchorage. It was black before we got clear, and I was cooking with just a dimmed headlamp so as not to disturb Dan's night vision, least he T-bone one of the floating pieces of ice, which by then were essentially invisible.

In the foggy black, guided only by the eerie pale shapes on our radar screen and plotter, we found a safe anchorage in the protection of a dot of an island, dropped the anchor, and shut everything down to savor the welcome silence.

When it was coffee time the next morning, we looked out at such a lovely and peaceful sight: the few acres of island just emerging from the dawn sun-lit fog, with seals popping up curiously around us, and the cry of crows and ravens in the trees.

"**Oct 6, 1982 - dawn, Frederick Sound, south of Mile 870:** We passed ice - small bergs and drift ice - on and off since midnight, starting south of Juneau. A sliver moon gave us just enough light to see the biggest bergs. Usually there is a chop, the waves phosphorescent as they break against the sides of the bergs. But then it got foggy, and my heart was in my throat - my pregnant wife is aboard, and most of a berg is underwater, and a berg the size of a car might only reveal a rounded shape a few inches above the surface, almost impossible to see even with the best radar.

If we were just a regular gill-netter or seiner traveling these waters, we'd have anchored up and waited for daylight. But we're deep in the water with 120,000 pounds of fish and the cannery wants them quick, so on we go. We turn off the compass light, the instruments, even the running lights to allow our eyes to get accustomed to the dark, to hope to see a berg in time.

A few years earlier, a friend was running in fog with another big load of fish, almost at his destination, the cannery town of Petersburg. He had a good radar, but it was a moonless night, spitting rain. The berg he hit probably wasn't much bigger than a fridge or a tub, totally invisible on radar. But it smashed in his wooden bow, and they sank with just enough time to jump into the skiff.

Top: running in and out of fog, 1975. Tender Northwind *in foreground,* Cypress *in distance.*
Right top: trying to get out of Le Conte at last light.
Right lower: the next morning: whew.. no ice in sight.

*The village visible east of **Mile 845** is **Kake**, a Tlingit native village, pop. around 600. A small fish processing facility provides markets for the local fishermen.*

*   **Mile 870** *is about the northern limit for icebergs that have drifted from Le Conte Glacier, 55 miles east.*

*   **Admiralty Island**, *larger than Long Is. NY, is the land mass to the west here. Mostly a National Monument and home to many brown bears. The Tlingit village of Angoon, pop 450, is on the island's west side.*

*   **Point Astley, mile 895**, *is a major sea lion rookery. We visited here in 2012, and counted almost 100 of the big bruisers.*

THE SMALL SHIP EXPERIENCE

Small ships offer a much more intimate experience than large ones. This is the *Wilderness Adventurer*, carrying about 50 passengers on a week-long cruise between Ketchikan and Juneau.

Typically such cruises will concentrate less on the ports and anchor up to explore places where passengers may hike and kayak, usually with no one else in sight. This was 2014, a particularly warm summer with just one sunny day after another.

Every morning we'd start with yoga on the back deck, have a great breakfast and head out for the activity of the day. It might be hiking, kayaking, snorkeling one day, even swimming for the hardy.

For information: Uncruise.com

Top: a platform on the boat's stern allows you to enter and exit your kayak on a flat, stable surface. Then the crew slowly slides you back into the water.

58

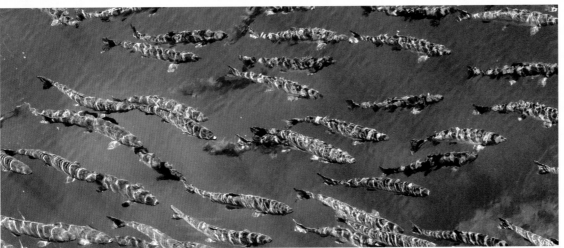

A friend grew up on a fox farm on **Harbor Island**, near **Mile 900**. When they hadn't caught enough salmon to feed the foxes, the father would send the kids over in the skiff to shoot a sea lion, cut it into pieces they could carry and bring it all back for the foxes.

In the 1970s and 80s, when I was operating fish boats in this area, ice from **Sawyer** and **Dawes Glaciers** were a menace to navigation in upper Stephens Passage. But today little ice gets out this far.

Top: we kayak near the face of Dawes Glacier. Note: photo taken with a telephoto lens, which makes the ice seem a lot closer. We actually kept a good quarter of a mile away, lest a calving berg create a wave big enough to capsize us.
Middle: pink salmon.
Lower: we get a kayak demo on the top deck on the way in to Misty Fjords.

Once I was in one of the ship's kayaks, in a creek mouth with thousands of salmon waiting to spawn. One of the guides saw what was happening and radioed to the ship where a couple was just relaxing in the hot tub after a long hike. Passing them flippers, snorkels, and masks, he told them to keep their bathing suits on and jump into the inflatible with him (this was a hot summer, and the creek waters were warm enough to swim.) He buzzed over to the creek where I was paddling and and they jumped in with the fish.

Of course the salmon were startled at first, but quickly got used to the snorkelers, who were treated to the stunning experience of being eye to eye with thousands of salmon!

Exploring:
Fords Terror

Little visited **Fords Terror** (named for a Navy crewman who, paddling into the inlet, was terrified by the violent tidal currents) is a dramatic fjord near regularly visited **Tracy Arm, Mile 900**. The tidal rapids in the entrance are dangerous to small craft and should only be attempted at slack water. I traveled there for the first time in my 32' salmon gillnetter:

"**Sept 5, 1972** - Just at 1, and with little water under us and at dead slow, we transited the rapids in the creek-like entrance to Fords Terror. Hardly spoke a word for the next mile, so dramatic was the scenery. The channel was scarcely a hundred feet wide. To the north a sheer rock wall rose a thousand feet before sloping back out of sight. To the south was a rocky beach rising rapidly to dark forests and snowy peaks. Old John Muir was the first white man here in the 1870s. He was so awed by the scenery he named it Yosemite Inlet, and don't think there have been too many visitor since. We passed a waterfall that was falling at least a hundred feet into the trees below. The gorge opened up to a basin perhaps a half mile by a half mile, and we dropped the hook and walked until our boat was just a dot on the far shore.

"The sun went over the mountain at 4:30 and the evening came early and chill. At dusk, flight after flight of ducks came in low and fast, to settle on the water near the shore with the rush of many wings and soft callings.

"Night came chilly, with northern lights again. Stood on the deck and watched the birds with Susanna until the cold drove us in. Yesterday and today, the places we visit make us feel small indeed."

"**Sept 6 - First frost!** The stove went out in the night and we woke to find the dog nestled in between us. To go out on the frosty deck on such a morning with the still, glassy basin around us, and dark forests and frozen hill above—words can't tell it, pictures can't show it."

THE BAD ICEBERG

In June of 2011, filmmaker Dan Kowalski and I found this stunning iceberg (lower photo on opposite page) at the mouth to Fords Terror, about 200' long with an arch 30' high. Now, Dan and I are very experienced; we know how suddenly and easily bergs can capsize. But we assumed this one, from where it was laying, was grounded and therefore stable.

Jumping in the small outboard inflatable skiff with our cameras, we circled that gorgeous iceberg in awe, stopped the engine and drifted, close to the arch, but being savvy guys, not underneath. It was a Zen-like experience: we could feel the berg's cold breath on our faces, hear the hiss of bubbles rising from the submerged mass below us. The blue translucent arch just towered over us, seemingly lit from within. The sea was still; in the distance was the whisper of the waterfall tumbling down the canyon wall: a magic moment.

Then there was this rumble that we felt more through the water than heard. Dan turned to me with a smile, "The iceberg is talking to us."

A moment later the iceberg broke in half, just at the top of the arch, almost directly over our heads. Stunned into inaction, our cameras hanging from our necks, we gasped as the nearer half rolled toward us, all in slow motion, smacking into the water just behind our outboard. Only when the other half rolled away and the previously underwater part emerged from the water under us, shoving water into our boat and pushing us back, did we have the presence of mind to start the motor and dart away, lest an ice projection catch our boat and flip it.

"Well," Dan said, when we'd gotten away from the now two bergs and caught our breath, "what was the worst that could have happened? We'd have been in the water, our cameras would have been toast, but we could have flipped the boat back over, and paddled the half mile back to where the *Sue Anne* was anchored and warmed up there..."

Or not, I thought...

So take it from a couple of really experienced guys: don't get close to icebergs in small craft!

Exploring:
Tracy Arm

Tracy Arm, a winding fjord close to Juneau, is both an alternate stop for ships unable to get a permit to visit Glacier Bay and a destination for Juneau-based excursions.

Many ships enter Tracy Arm early in order to make a port stop in Juneau later the same day. **Tip**: If your ship has a schedule like this, be sure to get up in time to see the entrance, and in particular the dramatic right-angle turn.

Also, look for glacial striations along the sides of the fjord. These are long scars or gouges parallel to the water that were created when rocks embedded in the glacier were carried with it as it moved down from the snow fields in the mountains, grinding grooves into the fjord walls.

Occasionally, because of fog or too much ice in Tracy Arm, ships will visit Endicott Arm to the south instead and get as close to the ice at Dawes Glacier as they can. Don't be disappointed: It is almost as dramatic as Tracy Arm; just a little farther from Juneau.

Top: What's wrong with this photo? (Except for no life jackets.. We were way too casual back then...) Actually, getting this close to a big iceberg is very risky, as they can roll over without warning, creating waves small enough to capsize small craft like this..

Left: passengers from a small ship explore the steep shore of Tracy Arm.

This bend is very dramatic in early morning light.

Icebergs sometimes ground on this gravel bar.

North Sawyer Glacier

Tracy Arm
1 inch = 5 miles

South Sawyer Glacier

900

Top: aboard the small ship Spirit of Oceanus, *you can see how steep the sides of the fjord are.*

Above: Entering Tracy Arm.

Right: don't try this at home.. Dogs don't like to be dropped off on little icebergs. He kept barking and barking until we returned and picked him up.

Downtown Juneau
and vecinity

Last Chance Basin and
Mining Museum

Flume Walking Trail

Governor's
Mansion

Cruise Ship Docks

JUNEAU

A bear? Behind the espresso stand? No roads in or out? You can only get there by boat or plane? What kind of a state capital is this?

Almost surrounded by high mountains and with a vast ice field—larger than Rhode Island—to the north, Juneau winters are substantially colder than that of Ketchikan or Sitka. Tlingit natives had fish camps near where downtown is today, but wintered in a more temperate and sheltered area near Auke Bay.

Alaska's first gold rush started here in 1880, but after the easy-to-find stream bed gold was gathered quickly, industrial-scale, deep tunnel mining was needed to follow the veins deep underground. Massive stamp mills were built to extract gold; it wasn't uncommon for 20 or more tons of ore to be dug and processed to yield a single ounce of fine gold. The tailings—the crushed rock that was left—were dumped along the shore, creating the flat land on which today's downtown Juneau was built.

At peak capacity, the big stamp mills of the Alaska-Juneau mine, still visible above the cruise-ship docks, could crush 12,000 tons of ore a day. Working conditions were dangerous. The entrance to the big Treadwell mine was nicknamed the "Glory Hole," for all the miners—sometimes one a week—that went to glory there. Eventually the gold played out, the tunnels—by then down to 2,100 feet below the channel—filled with water, and today all that's left are ruins and miles of tunnels.

If you see Build The Road bumper stickers around town, they're about a plan to build a road up the east side of Lynn Canal to connect to a ferry dock, where you could take a short ferry to Skagway, where there is a road out to the rest of the world. However, the geography is so steep and winter weather so challenging that it might not happen for a long while.

Right: young native lady and a ceremonial mask at a Juneau gallery.

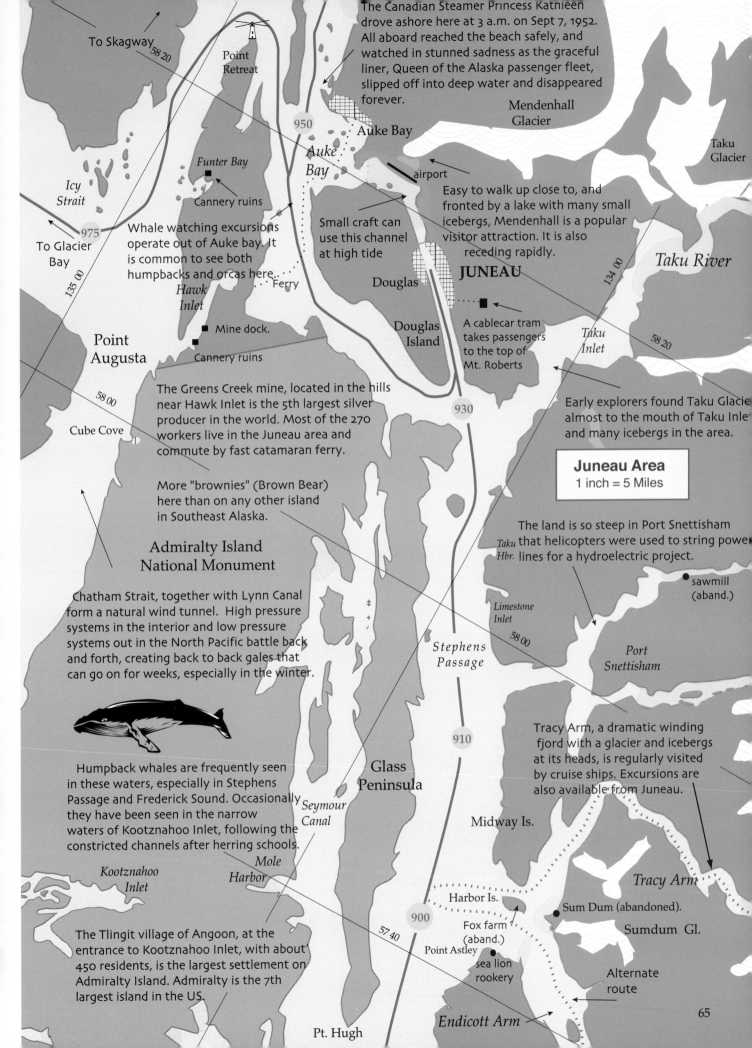

To Skagway

Point Retreat

The Canadian Steamer Princess Kathleen drove ashore here at 3 a.m. on Sept 7, 1952. All aboard reached the beach safely, and watched in stunned sadness as the graceful liner, Queen of the Alaska passenger fleet, slipped off into deep water and disappeared forever.

58 20

950

Mendenhall Glacier

Taku Glacier

Auke Bay

Auke Bay

Funter Bay

Cannery ruins

Icy Strait

airport

975

To Glacier Bay

135 00

Whale watching excursions operate out of Auke bay. It is common to see both humpbacks and orcas here.

Hawk Inlet

Ferry

Small craft can use this channel at high tide

Easy to walk up close to, and fronted by a lake with many small icebergs, Mendenhall is a popular visitor attraction. It is also receding rapidly.

Taku River

134 00

JUNEAU

Douglas

58 20

Taku Inlet

Mine dock.

Point Augusta

Douglas Island

Cannery ruins

A cablecar tram takes passengers to the top of Mt. Roberts

Taku Inlet

Early explorers found Taku Glacier almost to the mouth of Taku Inlet and many icebergs in the area.

58 00

The Greens Creek mine, located in the hills near Hawk Inlet is the 5th largest silver producer in the world. Most of the 270 workers live in the Juneau area and commute by fast catamaran ferry.

930

Cube Cove

Juneau Area
1 inch = 5 Miles

More "brownies" (Brown Bear) here than on any other island in Southeast Alaska.

The land is so steep in Port Snettisham that helicopters were used to string power lines for a hydroelectric project.

Taku Hbr.

sawmill (aband.)

Admiralty Island National Monument

Chatham Strait, together with Lynn Canal form a natural wind tunnel. High pressure systems in the interior and low pressure systems out in the North Pacific battle back and forth, creating back to back gales that can go on for weeks, especially in the winter.

Limestone Inlet

58 00

Port Snettisham

Stephens Passage

Humpback whales are frequently seen in these waters, especially in Stephens Passage and Frederick Sound. Occasionally they have been seen in the narrow waters of Kootznahoo Inlet, following the constricted channels after herring schools.

910

Glass Peninsula

Tracy Arm, a dramatic winding fjord with a glacier and icebergs at its heads, is regularly visited by cruise ships. Excursions are also available from Juneau.

Seymour Canal

Midway Is.

Kootznahoo Inlet

Mole Harbor

The Tlingit village of Angoon, at the entrance to Kootznahoo Inlet, with about 450 residents, is the largest settlement on Admiralty Island. Admiralty is the 7th largest island in the US.

900

57 40

Harbor Is.

Fox farm (aband.)

Point Astley

sea lion rookery

Sum Dum (abandoned).

Sumdum Gl.

Tracy Arm

Alternate route

Endicott Arm

Pt. Hugh

Juneau Excursions

(Subject to change)
Mendenhall Glacier Explorer
Mendenhall Gl. & Salmon Hatchery Tour
Original Alaska Salmon Bake
Underground Juneau
Rain forest Garden
A Taste of Juneau
Guide's Choice Adventure Hike
Dog Sled Summer Camp
Gold Panning & History Tour
Glacier View Bike & Brew
Rain forest Canopy & Zipline Expedition
Mountain Zipline & Rain forest Bike Ride
Juneau Sport-fishing Adventure
Juneau Steamboat Cruise
Photo Safari by Land & Sea
Alaska's Whales & Rain forest Trails
Whale Watching & Wildlife Quest
Mendenhall Glacier & Whale Quest
Whale Watching & Orca Point Lodge
Mendenhall Glacier Float Trip
Glacier View Sea Kayaking
Mendenhall Glacier Canoe Adventure
Taku Glacier Lodge Flight & Feast
Pilot's Choice Ice Age Exploration
Mendenhall Glacier Helicopter Tour
Four Glacier Adventure by Helicopter
Glacier & Dog Sled Adventure by Helicopter
Dog Sledding on the Mendenhall
Custom Hummer Adventure
Juneau Ice field Flightseeing

Top: tram upper station, Auke Bay in distance.
Left top: humpbacks are regularly seen here.
Left bottom: kayakers at Mendenhall Glacier.

Around Town

Top: this is the area where cruise ships tie up, circa 1910. The big building is the stamp mill, where the ore is crushed to extract the gold. *Juneau Douglas Museum*

Above: entrance to the maze of old mining tunnels that honeycomb the hills above and around Juneau.

Right: masked marcher at Celebration, the biannual Native festival in downtown Juneau in August, 2010. Tribes from all over SE Alaska gather to celebrate their culture. The highlights are performances by Native dancers and the parade.

MINING THE PILLARS:
THE COLLAPSE AT TREADWELL

The great Yukon Gold Rush was based on gold nuggets and gold dust being sifted out of streams and shallow pits: essentially surface gold. The men who rushed north in 1897 did so because they heard of individuals or small groups of guys "striking it rich."

The surface gold at Juneau was quickly found, but then large companies were created to follow the gold veins underground. This was industrial scale hard rock mining: thousands on thousands of tons of ore hauled from deep underground and crushed to separate the gold.

The method most commonly used was called pillar and room mining, in which ore was removed, creating vast underground rooms held up by untouched pillars of rock that would keep the ceiling from collapsing. Mines would have many levels of rooms, all held up by the columns of the room below.

The rooms in the Treadwell mine, above, on Douglas Island, across from Juneau, extended down to almost **2,000 feet, under the channel!** When the rich ore was exhausted, management decided to start 'mining the pillars' - shaving down the pillars of solid rock that actually held up the whole mine; not a particularly wise thing to do for obvious reasons.

Sure enough, occasionally a whole room would collapse when pillars failed after being weakened by shaving ore from them. Did this stop management from continuing to mine the pillars? Noooo. Next buildings around the mine began to settle, then a crack in the earth opened and almost swallowed the big steel pool by the clubhouse. And still they kept shaving them pillars... Finally a crack opened in the earth close to the shore of the channel and the maze of tunnels, rooms, and pillars quickly flooded, never to open again, and the First World War was waiting for all the laid off workers.

Top: Treadwell Mine, circa 1910, downtown Juneau opposite shore on left.
Right: old sign in the Last Chance Basin Mining Museum.

SIGNALS
1 BELL....HOIST
1 " ....STOP IF IN MOTION
2 BELLS..LOWER
3 " ....MEN ON RUN SLOW
7 " ....ACCIDENT HOIST OR LOWER BY VERBAL ORDER
3-2-1 " ....READY TO SHOOT
ENGINEER SHALL AFTER SIGNAL 3-2-1 RAISE BUCKET OF CAGE TWO FEET AND LOWER AGAIN AND SHALL REMAIN AT HI POST UNTIL FINAL SIGNAL IS GIVEN AND COMMAND EXECUTE

LEVELS

1-1 BELLS 1ST LEVEL		4-1 BELLS 11TH LEVEL	
1-2 " 2ND "		4-2 " 12TH "	
1-3 " 3RD "		4-3 " 13TH "	
1-4 " 4TH "		4-4 " 14TH "	
1-5 " 5TH "		4-5 " 15TH "	
2-1 " 6TH "		5-1 " 16TH "	
2-2 " 7TH "		5-2 " 17TH "	
2-3 " 8TH "		5-3 " 18TH "	
2-4 " 9TH "		5-4 " 19TH "	
2-5 " 10TH "		5-5 " 20TH "	

RULES GOVERNING SIGNALS.
RULE I. IN GIVING ORDINARY SIGNALS MAKE STROKES ON BELL AT REGULAR INTERVALS SIMILAR TO "READY TO SHOOT" 3-2-1 BELLS, EACH BAR (-) MUST TAKE THE SAME TIME AS EACH STROKE OF THE BELL

FLIGHTSEEING CHOICES:

DON'T MISS GETTING UP IN THE
AIR!

Alaska has some truly spectacular scenery, and the best way to see more than you'll see from a ship or around the towns is to get up into the air. Fortunately there are flightseeing excursions in all the towns that your ship will be stopping at, except Icy Strait Point and Sitka (although private air charters can be arranged in both places.)

Ketchikan flightseeing focuses on nearby Misty Fjords, while both Juneau and Skagway offer both floatplane flightseeing, and helicopter tours, which land and allow passengers to walk around a glacier.

Top: view over Juneau Ice Field. Above: an Otter floatplane waits for passengers.
Right: on a Skagway area glacier.

Pt.Lena, Mile 951, was the last resting place for the crack liner, Princess Kathleen. She ran ashore in 1957. All climbed down to shore, but the graceful liner slipped off into deep water.

Sentinel Island, Mile 962 was almost the end of the graceful steamer Princess May as well. She ran ashore in 1910, but no one was injured and she was repaired and returned to service.

Vanderbilt Reef, Mile 966, was the site of the 1917 loss of the Princess Sophia. On her last run of the season, in a blinding snow-storm she drove up on the reef. Rescue boats arrived to take passengers off, but the ship seemed stable, so the Sophia's captain decided to wait for better weather. Bad choice: the wind drove the ship off the reef in the night, drowning all 243 souls.

Upton's Log

"Lynn Canal, Oct. 2, 1973 - Comes with NW gale driving down off the vast cold mainland to the north. Sleet turned to snow after midnight, blotting out the lights of the boats around us. Picked up net at first light in driving snow, ice building up on the corkline. But it had almost a hundred salmon; that's a thousand bucks that looks mighty good in February. My wife stays inside when I pick the net on these really nasty nights, cozy with the dog on the bunk, don't blame her.

"Picked last set up before noon in stinging snow, had to turn away from the wind and just wait for squalls to pass. The wind was blowing the tops off the seas and slopping them into the cockpit. So glad to finally get net all in, get inside, and change into dry clothes by the cozy stove. Wipers froze and started making ice on the rigging as well.

"Bucked at half speed for three hours before the land came out of the snow with two fish buying boats snuggled up against the shore, their decklights on in mid-afternoon, the hills behind disappearing in snowsqualls. We the last boat to unload, then they were gone, lost almost at once in the gloom and swirling snow, 200 miles to go to the cannery.

"Ran up to the head of the cove and tied alongside three friends with all our anchors out. Night came quick with 15 boats crowded into this tiny anchorage. Weather wild out there, but cozy enough in here with salmon baking, S. beside me and the good doggie snoring on the floor. Violent squalls again at 9, laying us all over with their power, lines and fenders creaking."

More than any other waterway in Southeast Alaska, Lynn Canal is a wind tunnel. The southern part of the Canal opens directly into Chatham Strait, creating this 200 mile long canyon. North Pacific lows roar up from the south and Alaska Interior highs roar down from the north. The effect is that sometimes you get a nasty gale from the south followed by an equally nasty gale from the north with hardly any time in between. But if you're on a cruise ship, no worries; summers are usually gale-free.

Top: Princess May; see text on left.
Right: fish buying vessel with salmon gillnetters alongside, Chilkat Inlet, Mile 994N.

Glacier Bay lies beyond these mountains.

Chilkat Inlet

Port Chilkoot

Haines

Lynn Canal

Looking west from
Mile 1018N

We are Not like Skagway

We get very few ship dockings
We are self-owned shops
We are not owned by the cruise lines

Please help support Haines!

Upper Lynn Canal *has some very dramatic scenery. The closer you get to Skagway, the better it gets. Early morning light can be especially dramatic, so if you're headed into Skagway, consider setting your alarm for 5:30, and going out on deck with your camera.*

Mile 1010N - near here is the proposed ferry terminal that would be at the end of the road from Juneau. Have a look at the steep hillsides and imagine how it would be to keep the road open in winter, with snow roaring down the many avalanche chutes. This is why it is unlikely that the road will be built anytime soon.

Though just 10 miles south of Skagway, Haines and Port Chilkoot, just walking distance from each other, are a world apart from Skagway and its often 6 or 8,000 visitors a day.

Haines is pretty much small town Alaska with the Southeast Alaska State Fair in late July, and the Chilkat Bald Eagle Preserve Gathering beginning in October and going on for most of the winter. This is when it seems like all the Eagles in Alaska (one estimate was 4,000!) gather to chow down on dog salmon, which spawn in the nearby Chilkat River, and die shortly thereafter. In 2011, for example, around 360,000 10 pound chum salmon spawned here. That's about 90 fish per eagle: plenty of chow...

What looks like a college town at the head of the cruise ship dock is Port Chilkoot, which used to be an Army base. Today there is a native arts center, a craft liquor distillery, restaurant, and shops .

Popular activities for visitors are biking, kayaking, river rafting, and just enjoying a little more peace and quiet than you are used to in the other towns! Or... if you want to get to Skagway... jump on the fast ferry!

Left top: braided Chilkat River Channels.
Lower: in the Alaska Indian Arts Center at Port Chilkoot. Note eagles on trees in photograph!

71

"Them days it was every man for hisself. **The faster a boat could get out of (Skagway), the faster it could get back to Seattle or Vancouver and pick up another load of suckers.**"

ISLANDER

"For some the challenge of The North - the cold, the conditions, was simply too much:

"It was a real cold night. We walked along in the snow and we come to a fellow setting on the back of a Yukon sled. Yep, he was sitting there in the middle of the road talking to hisself. He looked plumb played out. He never seen us: he just went on talking to hisself. Over and over he'd say: 'It's hell. Yes; multiply it by ten and then multiply that by ten, and that ain't half as bad as this is. Yes, it's hell...'"
- Martha Mckeown, *The Trail Led North*

GOLD, GOLD, GOLD! The news spread across the country like a prairie fire: total greenhorns staggering off the steamers in Seattle, barely able to drag their gold-filled suitcases. Machinists dropped their tools, farmers dropped the reins of their horses. On the day the word got to New York City, train tickets to Seattle sold out almost immediately. Within a few weeks, almost a hundred thousand, mostly men, were on the move.

 Along the Seattle and Vancouver waterfronts merchants set up shop, offering everything a would be Klondiker might need. Badly rotten ships with barely functioning engines were resurrected, filled with the hopeful, and headed north to Alaska.

A thousand miles north of Seattle, they approached Skagway. The view, that fall of 1897, was humbling: the narrowing channel bounded by steep rock walls rising to ice and snow. The realization of what the men might soon be facing began to sober them.

The first step was getting ashore and over the passes. Canadian authorities (the gold strike was in Canada) required each person to bring supplies for a full year - essentially about a ton of food and equipment - carried up to the top of the pass one backbreaking load at a time. One prospector reported that so many folks were on the trail that if you stepped out of line to rest (from carrying your 60 or 70 pound pack) it might be 15 minutes before there would even be a break in the line so that you could step back in.

The whole trip over the passes and on to the next major stop, Lake Bennett, was grueling, to say the least.

Left top, the Islander, *filled to capacity and beyond with prospectors-to-be.*
Left, bottom left: Men with the boats they built at Lake Bennett. AM b64-1-43
Top: Old number 73, one of the original steam engines to carry Klondikers over White Pass, still pulls excursion trains to the top of the pass. By the time the line was completed in 1900, the gold rush to the Klondike was essentially over.
Left: the "Golden Staircase" over Chilkoot Pass in the late fall of 1897. Native porters made a good living carrying loads up and over the pass to the shores of Lake Bennett. A number of cable tramways were built to help get the heavy loads to the summit. UW Hegg 100

"Some leaked, some didn't steer. They had lots of things wrong with them, But a lot of the boats, made of whipsawed lumber, had beautiful lines and sailed as pretty as anything I ever did see on the Columbia.

Yes, sir, that was an expedition, that fleet of boats getting ready to set out from Lake Bennett, come spring of '98"

– Martha McKeown, The Trail Led North

A tent city sprang up next to the frozen lake, and the men cut trees, sawed them into planks, built boats, and waited for spring and ice out. Next was the 500 mile trip down the Yukon, through the dreaded White Horse Rapids, and finally to Dawson, and the Klondike.

And then the unexpected: they arrived to find that the good claims had been taken before most of the men even left their homes. Of the 100,000 that left their homes headed north, maybe 30,000 actually made it all the way to Dawson. Of those, just a handful 'struck it rich.' Most worked for someone else, made a little money and moved on, either back home, or to another gold rush (there were several).

Yet their adventure transcends time. All experienced the powerful drama of The North. Those who returned, even penniless, brought back stories to entertain generations of breathless children and grandchildren.

It is the drama of 1897 and '98 that fills this town. Skagway blossomed for few years, lawless and rough, and then almost disappeared. Yet, surprisingly, it survived. Today, the town still retains its charm and the ghosts of the men who passed through in the epic Klondike Gold Rush still walk these streets.

Those gaunt-faced men have moved on to whatever fate The North had in store for them. But the town the boom built at the jumping-off place for the Klondike remains, historically important and looking much as it did then, when some 80 saloons and many professional women served the lonely men on their way north.

Skagway was essentially built between 1897 and 1900. It was the weather that kept the turn of the century buildings intact. Buildings that would have rotted away without maintenance in rainy Ketchikan, endured longer in this much drier, sunnier climate.

Today, Skagway offers a unique experience to visitors. Even the vegetation and climate is different from the rest of Southeast Alaska because the town is under the influence of the harsher temperature extremes of the interior instead of the milder, wetter, maritime climate elsewhere in the region.

Skagway can get very busy. It is a not-to-be-missed town, but if you are a repeat passenger and are ready for something a little quieter, a fast ferry (45 minutes, $68 round-trip) can take you to Haines and historic Port Chilkoot, where there are some pleasant walks, a few galleries, and restaurants overlooking Lynn Canal.

Pick up a copy of the walking tour map at the AB Hall. It's got directions up to the Gold Rush Cemetery, the Trail of '98 Museum, and other points of interest. It's definitely worthwhile to walk around with the map as your guide.

Of course, Skagway's signature hike is up the old Chilkoot Trail. This is way, way more than a pleasant stroll; more like a grueling four- to five-day epic, and that's in summer, not in the depth of winter with the poorly insulated clothing of the day and 2,000 pounds of gear to pack over the summit. If you start up the trail, think about this: many of the men who used the trail made a dozen or more trips back and forth to ferry their loads or hired a Native porter.

Dyea was the start of the Chilkoot Trail. Not much is left now; Skagway boomed, Dyea died. Though Klondikers came ashore at Dyea; today the town is far from the water, due to glacial re-bound. This occurs for centuries after glaciers have receded: the land, no longer carrying the immense weight of a glacier, slowly rises up. Even though the rise at Dyea is only about three-quarters of an inch a year, in the 114 years since the Gold Rush, the land has risen seven feet, enough to push the waterfront a good quarter-mile back.

Top: downtown.. must be supper time (hardly anyone on the streets!)

Right: just a sampling of the many restaurants and specialty shops here.

Opposite top: the fleet of home made boats leaving Lake Bennett after ice out, spring, 1897. Some 6,000 boat were hand build on the shores of the frozen lake over the winter. Yukon Archives

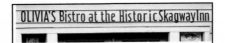

An early September afternoon, 1973. I am a commercial salmon fisherman, just my wife and I on our little 32' fish boat. We have four days off between fishing periods in Chilkat Inlet, near Haines. Together with a dozen or so other boats, all friends, we steam up to Skagway for the weekend.

Our group might be 25 total. But when the Skagway locals see us steaming into the harbor the word goes out: "Customers; gotta' stay open longer. " And so the few restaurants and shops of this town of 800 stayed open for our little group. It's not like that anymore..

Revenue for the railroad in those days depended totally on a Canadian mine that shipped its ore by rail to the port at Skagway, to be put on ships that took the ore to a smelter in Tacoma. Back then the busiest days in Skagway were the twice weekly arrivals of the Alaska state ferry with a few hundred passengers. The railroad even closed down in 1982, when ore prices dropped.

Then along came the Alaska cruise industry, a few small ships at first, quickly growing into a whole new economy for Southeast Alaska. For Skagway it meant that the railroad would reopen and transform itself, with classic freight cars barged in from all over the country, refurbished and put back to use hauling cruise ship passengers, into the most popular shore excursion in all of Alaska.

Of course, when a town of 800 has to accommodate 10,000 visitors a day for most of the summer, along with the seasonal workers to support them, things, like housing especially, get stretched pretty thin. If you walk around town, you'll notice a lot of campers, tents, and old school buses used for housing, making for a pretty fun social scene for all the young workers.

Right: Dennis Corrington and one of the wonderful pieces of native art in his store, Corrington's Alaska Ivory, offers, along with an unusual free museum.

SKAGWAY EXCURSIONS

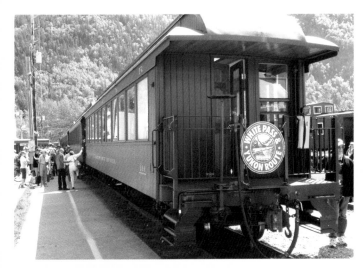

(Subject to change)
Skagway & the Dangerous Days of '98
Klondike Summit & Liarsville Experience
Klondike Summit, Bridge, & Salmon Bake
Historical Tour & Liarsville Salmon Bake
Skagway's Original Street Car
To the Summit
Experience the Yukon
White Pass Scenic Railway
Best of Skagway
Klondike Scenic Highlights
Delectable Jewell Gardens
Deluxe Klondike Experience & Rail Adventure
Alaska Garden & Gourmet Tour
Yukon Jeep Adventure
Horseback Riding Adventure
Klondike Bicycle Tour
Rainforest Bicycle Tour

Klondike Rock Climbing & Rappelling
Alaska Sled Dog & Musher's Camp
Chilkoot Trail Hike & Float Adventure
Glacier Point Wilderness Safari
Glacier Lake Kayak & Scenic Railway
Dog Sledding & Glacier Flightseeing
Glacier Discovery By Helicopter
Heli-Hike & Rail Adventure
Alaska Nature & Wildlife Expedition
Remote Coastal Nature Hike
Takshanuk Mountain Trail by 4x4
Eagle Preserve Wildlife River Adventure
Chilkoot Lake Freshwater Fishing
Wilderness Kayak Experience
Skagway's Custom Classic Cars
Glacier Country Flightseeing

Exploring:
John Muir and Glacier Bay

Imagine you're John Muir, an amateur geologist, in 1879. You're sure Yosemite's valleys were carved by ice, but no one believes you. You've heard a rumor that there were glaciers in faraway Alaska, take the steamer to Wrangell, hire some native paddlers in a big cedar canoe. You ask them to take you to the bay of big ice, but no one is really sure where it is except somewhere to the north.

And so in mid-October, they set out, crossing rough channels, sleeping in Indian villages. Arriving at the bay itself, they found a band of

seal hunters from the village of Hoonah, persuaded one to come as a guide. The guide frightened Muir's paddlers with tales of friends who had drowned when icebergs came up from underwater and capsized their canoes. But Muir charmed them into continuing on and so entered Glacier Bay at last, which had emerged from the ice within the lifetime of his guide. He was stunned by what he found and immediately knew that what he saw confirmed his Yosemite theories, which were then reluctantly accepted by geologists.

Muir's discovery and what he wrote about it drew the first real tourists to Alaska, passengers on the big steamship *Queen* and others. They would go right up to the face of the mighty Muir Glacier which in those days was calving 10-15 big bergs an hour!!! Not only that but they would land passengers ashore and put up ladders to the top of the glacier face so that passengers could climb up and walk around!

Top: steamer Queen, 1898. Muir's elegiac descriptions of Glacier Bay in-spired the first cruise ships to visit Alaska. Drawing by Christine Cox.
Right: above Muir Glacier, 1893. American Geographical Society.

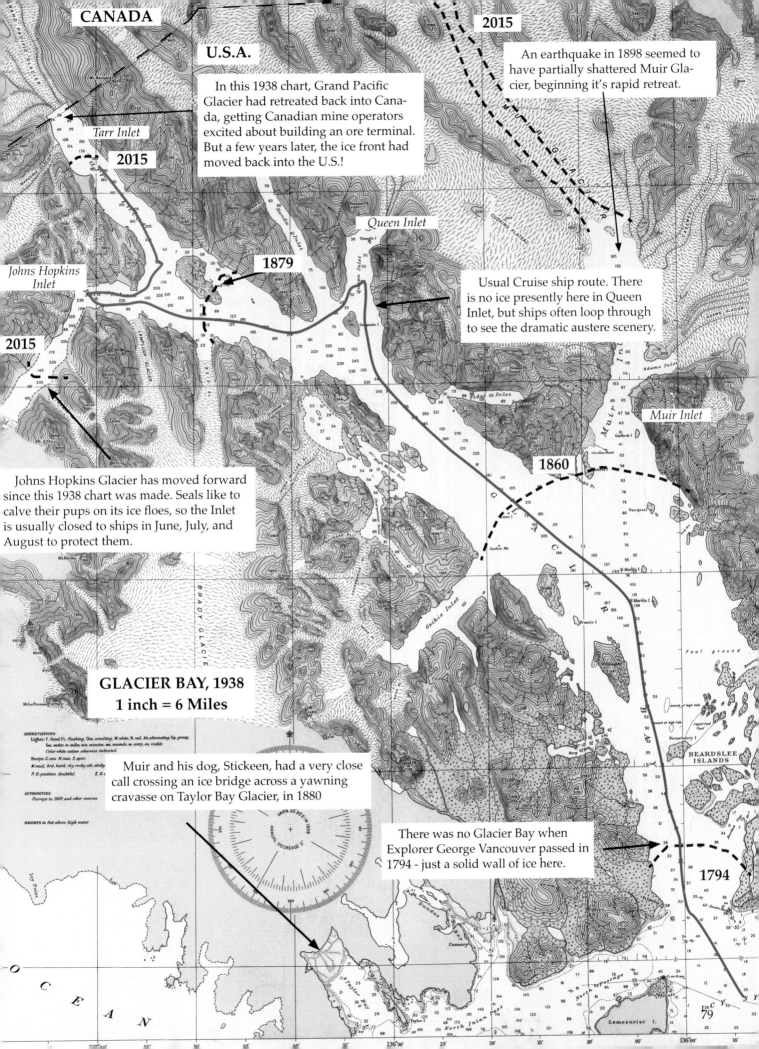

CANADA

U.S.A.

2015

In this 1938 chart, Grand Pacific Glacier had retreated back into Canada, getting Canadian mine operators excited about building an ore terminal. But a few years later, the ice front had moved back into the U.S.!

An earthquake in 1898 seemed to have partially shattered Muir Glacier, beginning it's rapid retreat.

Tarr Inlet

2015

Johns Hopkins Inlet

2015

Queen Inlet

1879

Usual Cruise ship route. There is no ice presently here in Queen Inlet, but ships often loop through to see the dramatic austere scenery.

Muir Inlet

1860

Johns Hopkins Glacier has moved forward since this 1938 chart was made. Seals like to calve their pups on its ice floes, so the Inlet is usually closed to ships in June, July, and August to protect them.

GLACIER BAY, 1938
1 inch = 6 Miles

ABBREVIATIONS
Lights: F. fixed. Fl. flashing. Occ. occulting. W. white. R. red. Alt. alternating. Gp. group.
Sec. sector. m. miles. min. minutes. sec. seconds. ev. every. vis. visible
Color white unless otherwise indicated.
Buoys: C. can. N. nun. S. spar.
M. mud. hrd. hard. rky. rocky. stk. sticky.
P. D. position doubtful.   E.D.

AUTHORITIES
Surveys to 1907 and other sources

HEIGHTS in feet above high water

Muir and his dog, Stickeen, had a very close call crossing an ice bridge across a yawning crevasse on Taylor Bay Glacier, in 1880

There was no Glacier Bay when Explorer George Vancouver passed in 1794 - just a solid wall of ice here.

1794

BEARDSLEE ISLANDS

O C E A N

KAYAKERS, LAMPUGH GLACIER:
WOULD YOU CAMP HERE?

When your ship enters lower Glacier Bay at about **Mile 1005**, you could be excused for asking, "So, where's the ice?" Well, in the 250 or so years (just the blink of an eye in geologic time) since the first white men saw the bay, most of the ice has disappeared and you'll have to travel almost 50 miles to get to the ice front.

The first ships always went to Muir Glacier, with a front around 200 feet high <u>calving off **big** bergs at the rate of about 10 or 15 an hour!</u> Today consider yourself lucky if you see one major calving event. Also before there were so many cruise ships that the Park Service that manages Glacier Bay had to institute rules, ships would blast their big air horns which would sometimes dislodge enough ice for a dramatic photo. Today a cruise ship that did that might get fined or even banned.

Top: the front wall of a glacier is unstable, as the fresh icefall in the pix shows. Probably not a good idea to camp too close.
Right: an apartment-spire topples into the water.
Above: probably 50 years ago, this glacier in John's Hopkins Inlet calved bergs.

Top: Brown bear claws mussels off the rocks. Keep your binoculars handy. Bears are likely to appear on the hillsides above the bay as moving dots, as they gather berries. If the tide is low, you may see them along the shore as well. Ki Whorton

Left: For reasons not fully understood, Glacier Bay is also an excellent place for whale-watching. If you are exceptionally lucky you may see a breach like this one. Minden Pictures

Left, bottom: Seals are commonly seen on ice floes throughout Glacier Bay. So many use the ice calving from John Hopkins Glacier to birth their young that part of the bay is closed during the summer. If your ship goes in there, consider yourself lucky, as it is one of the most dramatic areas in the whole Bay. DK

Below: Look on the steepest slopes for mountain goats like this one. You will be surprised at their ability to move around on incredibly steep terrain. DK

Exploring:
Hoonah and Icy Strait Point

Top: Like many Alaska small towns, the fish plant is the main economic driver. These are trollers at Hoonah Cold Storage on a gorgeous summer evening.

Left: early photos around Hoonah.

Opposite top: A zipline rider with Icy Strait Point (the old Hoonah Packing Company cannery) below. This particular zip has six parallel lines and is the longest ride of any zipline in Alaska. The ride ends at a restaurant, so you can catch a bite as well.

Opposite left: There is a pleasant short walk through the rain forest between the Cannery and the Landing Zone Bar and Grill. Easy wide path, definitely worth doing!

A CANNERY TURNED INTO A VISITOR ATTACTION..
WHAT WOULD THE OLD-TIMERS HAVE SAID?

When it opened in 2003, Icy Strait Point was unique among Alaska cruise ports. Ship visits are limited to one at a time, and the facility—a renovated cannery next to a Tlingit Indian village—is surrounded by wilderness. If you've cruised Alaska before, you know how congested the other towns can be with four or five ships in port at once. A visit here is a welcome change.

Passengers come ashore by lighter. The main feature is the cannery dock, which has a museum, cafe/restaurant, and numerous shops. Cannery life was a major cultural and economic element in coastal Alaska, and this is an excellent chance to get a close look. There are walking trails and a shuttle bus to nearby Hoonah, the largest Tlingit village in Alaska. The facility is owned by a Native corporation, which has preserved the rich Tlingit culture throughout.

Icy Strait Point is located in Port Frederick, just across Icy Strait from the entrance to Glacier Bay.

WHERE RUSSIA BECAME AMERICA

Consider yourself lucky if your ship stops here. The lack of a cruise ship dock (all but very small cruise ships anchor and use lighters to send passengers ashore) and a location slightly off the beaten path make for a more mellow downtown than Ketchikan, Juneau, or Skagway.

Sitka was the capital when Alaska was part of Russia from the late 1700s until 1867. With brutal efficiency, sometimes slaughtering whole villages of natives if they didn't hunt for them, the Russians forced natives to hunt and kill sea otters for their valuable fur. Those furs created an empire that stretched from the Aleutians all the way down to Northern California.

Those were good years when Sitka was the busiest port on the Northwest Coast. Its residents drank fine wines and enjoyed ballet, when Ketchikan was a native village and Juneau was ice and snow.

After the Russians slaughtered the sea otters almost to extinction, and Moscow was humiliated by Britain and France in the Crimean war in the 1850s, Russia was almost broke, and approached the US about selling Alaska. It was a great deal for the US: $7.2 million, about 2 cents an acre, done in 1867.

However the purchase was ridiculed as Seward's Folly or Seward's Icebox (William Seward being the Secretary of State at the time). Critics were silenced when gold was discovered.

After the Americans took over, Sitka slowly evolved into a sleepy fishing and logging town on the ocean side of Baranof Island.

In more modern times, Sitka's economy depended on the big plywood mill out in Sawmill Cove, and on commercial fishing. The closure of the mill in 1992 was a major financial blow to the town. But instead of languishing, Sitka experienced a slow renaissance based on the arts and, to a lesser degree, tourism.

Today, having missed the booms and busts of the gold rush, Sitka has become the cultural center of SE Alaska.

Top: view to the south from Castle Hill.
Right: salmon gill net crews - Sitka is a major commercial fishing center.

Top: snowy owl at Raptor Center, where injured owls, eagles, and hawks are cared for after being injured. Those that heal completely are often released into the wild. Those with injuries that prevent them from flying again are often sent to zoos or other wildlife centers, while others live on at the center.

Left; new old old totems at the Sitka National Historical Park, a short walk to the east along the shore from where passengers come ashore from ships.

Far left: a young cookie vendor - with many fewer vistors, the retail scene in Sitka is much mellower than in either Juneau, Skagway, or Ketchikan.

Sitka is one of those places where you really need to get out on the water. On the outside coast, yet protected by a screen of islands, it's close to good fishing, whale watching, excellent kayaking, and other activities on the water. Fortunately there are excursions offering all of these activities and more.

For walkers there's a really nice one - just turn right along the shore and follow the sidewalk to the Sitka National Historical Park with carving shed, and a totem walk with the poles set here and there in the forest. Pick up a map at the park, walk the totem trail to Sawmill Creek Rd. turn left, go about a hundred yards and take the driveway up to the Raptor Center. Then on the way back you can stop in at the Sheldon Jackson Museum.

If you turn left coming ashore and follow the shore, and work your way under the bridge that leads to the airport, you'll come upon fish processing row, with numerous cold storage plants processing crab, salmon, and halibut. Then turning around, you can return through downtown to the dock again: if you do both those walks, you will have pretty much done Sitka.

Top: Russian Orthodox congregation inspects model of their new church, around 1840.

Opposite right: native trio; white shirts probably made of muskrat skins. Photos from E.W. Merrill Collection, Sitka National Historical Park

A VOLCANIC PRANK

Mount Edgecumbe looms over Sitka, a prominent landfall in the days when ships from Asia came to load plywood from the now-closed mill. The volcano has been dormant for about 4,000 years.

Early on April Fool's Day, 1974, local prankster "Porky" Bickar loaded around 100 old car tires into a helicopter and flew up to the top of the volcano in pre dawn darkness, set them alight to create a dramatic smoky fire, and spray-painted "Happy April Fool's Day" in 50-foot letters around the crater. Then he flew back to town and spread the word that Mount Edgecumbe was erupting.

SITKA EXCURSIONS

(Subject to change)

Russian America History Tour
Russian America & Raptor Center Tour
Sitka Nature & History Walk
Sitka Bike & Hike Tour
Advanced Bike Adventure
Tongass Rain forest Hike
4x4 Wilderness Adventure
Sitka Sport-fishing
Wilderness Sea Kayaking Adventure
Dry Suit Snorkel Adventure
Sea Life Discovery Semi-Submersible
Sea Otter & Wildlife Quest
Sea Otter Quest & Alaska Raptor Center
Silver Bay Nature Cruise & Hatchery Tour
Wildlife Quest & Beach Trek
Alaska Up-Close Exclusive Cruise Adventure

Exploring:
Peril Strait and the wild outside coast

The 60 or so miles of coast south of Sitka, all the way to Cape **Ommaney, Mile 750W** are a series of rugged headlands and long, deep, and narrow bays leading far into the interior. Due to the ruggedness of the country, except for an occasional fish boat or passing yacht, the land is vast and lonely.

Dramatic 3.271' **Mt. Edgecumbe, Mile 818W**, an extinct volcano, is a major landmark.

The western portion of Chichagof Island, from Peril Strait to Cross Sound is all a National Scenic Area, and protected from most future development.

Peril Strait is a winding shortcut between Sitka, on the outside coast, and the more protected inner waters of Chatham Strait. Here the tide runs strongly enough to suck the big Coast Guard navigational buoys completely underwater.

The Alaska ferry *LeConte* hit a rock here in 2004 and almost sank. It was Sitka's main ship connection to the 'outside' and was out of service for much of the season. Electronic glitch with the navigation equipment? Nope, human error...

Top: western part of Peril Strait from about 25,000 feet. Rock ferry hit is near the two islands beneath aircraft wing.

Right: ferry *LeConte* in Peril Strait in better days, near the exact spot where she was to become impaled on a rock a few years later.

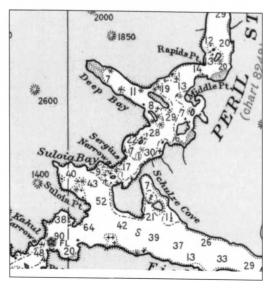

88

An active fleet of commercial salmon trollers operates out of Tenakee.

Top: **Rosie's Blue Moon Cafe** was a lot busier when the cannery was running and the loggers were in town. But sometimes it was got rough: "They alla time wanna fight," said Rosie.

Upper left: Alaska kids are tough; this was the last week of May, and they were swimming. Not dipping... swimming.

Upper right: unloading the Alaska Seaplane Beaver. The load that day was frozen goods for the store, a tire for a four wheeler, a big solar panel, and mail that was a sack of letters and about 20 Amazon boxes.

Once it was cannery workers that filled the long row of south facing waterfront houses. Then the cannery closed, and it became more of a summer and weekend community for folks flying out from Juneau.

Fortunately, in 2015, at least, there were still enough students for the State to fund a teacher, and thereby allowing families with children to stay, a critical component of small town life.

The tidy covered hot spring in the center of town makes the long winter go a lot easier.

Cape Spencer Light-house, Mile 1035, is the end of the Inside Passage. Mariners: tie things down before heading further north.

The entrance to Lituya Bay, Mile 1075, is dangerous and has claimed many vessels.

Mile 1075

Caution: breakers have been observed as much as two miles from shore off Dry Bay, Mile 1105.

The entrance to Dangerous River, Mile 1150, should only be attempted by small craft, at high tide, with local knowledge.

Top: Dawn Princess off Cape Saint Elias, Mile 1310, a major landmark along this coast.

Mariners tread cautiously here. They know they will not find harbors with easy access when the wind blows, except for a few bays just north of Cape Spencer. This is the outside coast: bold, rugged, and flanked by the windy Gulf of Alaska on one side and the stunning and rugged St. Elias Range on the other. Take the time to go on deck with your binoculars. No other coast in North America is like this.

Look for **La Perouse Glacier, Mile 1060**. With its almost perpendicular 200- to 300-foot face, it's an outstanding landmark along this section of coast. This is an active glacier. As recently as 1997, it was advancing into the ocean, after having receded far enough to allow foot passage across the face at low tide.

To the east is mostly wilderness, a vast region from the coast up over the Fairweather Range and into Canada's Yukon Territory almost to the Alaska Highway.

East and north of Hubbard Glacier is an area that has been nicknamed "The Roof of North America"—an immense rock, ice, and snow world with many of the continent's highest peaks. Ten thousand-footers are common here, and there are at least four higher than 15,000'.

Much of this area is the Wrangell-St. Elias National Park and Wilderness. This mountain wall catches the wet, eastward-flowing air, creating heavy snow. The immense weight of the snow pack creates the largest glaciers on the entire Pacific coast, part of a vast ice mass that extends parallel to the coast in an unbroken line, except for two places, almost 400 miles to Anchorage.

1800' high tidal wave started here

TERROR IN LITUYA BAY

When something awakened commercial fisherman Howard Ulrich the evening of August 9, 1958, he stared out his window in amazement. The mountains at the head of the bay were jumping in an earthquake that knocked the needle off a seismograph in Seattle, 1,000 miles away. Next, an entire mountainside collapsed, creating a tidal wave that stripped the forest across the fjord to bare rock up to 1,800 feet above sea level!

As he watched, the tidal wave, having settled to "only" 50 feet high, headed for his anchored boat. Putting a life jacket on his six-year-old, he started the engine and headed directly into the wave. Luckily, his anchor chain snapped and the wave carried him over the trees on the spit, and out into the Pacific. Another boat sank, but the crew was rescued. A third disappeared; all aboard were lost.

Now mariners who stop in here wonder: 'Can it happen again?'

90

"**Something woke me deep in the night**, and I sat up in my bunk suddenly, listening. The engine of our king crab boat was just idling long - that was odd; but it was something else that had woken me. Then the boat took a sudden roll and I felt it; our motion was slow and loggy, very unlike the quick roll she'd had when I went to sleep. Up in the pilothouse I saw the problem as soon as I looked out the window: ice. Though we were five miles from land, the bitter wind flowing down the Copper River valley had chilled every part of our boat so that the spray flung up by the sea had become a thick layer of ice, making our boat dangerously topheavy. We didn't have to be told what to do: we knew that if we didn't beat off the ice and shovel it over the side quick, we would capsize before morning.

"Without a word, we suited up in hooded snowmobile suits. Another crewman and I inched out onto the bow, where the 2" diameter pipe rails around the bow had become so thick, they were growing together into a solid wall of ice. With baseball bat and hammer we broke ice off the rails and anchor winch, kicking the pieces over the side. Once the bow dipped deep into a big sea, and we were instantly waist deep in swirling water that pulled at us before suddenly clearing away as the bow rose again.

"Only after two long hours did the boat seem to ride a little higher, roll a little quicker. But we knew that if the wind picked up even more, it would make ice faster than we could knock it off and we'd have to turn around, and run downwind out into the ocean, away from the bitter land breeze.

"It's the Copper River Wind, boy," the mate told me. "All that air just gets frozen up there and rolls straight down the valley to the ocean."

- Bering Sea Blues, by Joe Upton

Hubbard Glacier *lies at the head of Yakutat Bay, **Mile 1165**. It is only occasionally visited by cruise ships, usually those which have been unable to get a permit to visit Glacier Bay.*

***Malaspina Glacier, Mile 1200**, is about the size of the state of Rhode Island.*

*When Captain Cook passed **Mile 1210** in 1776, he found a tongue of ice sticking several miles out into the ocean. Since then, the ice has retreated back into **Icy Bay**.*

Mile 1310 ▷

*Salmon gillnet vessels from Cordova in Prince William Sound harvest the well known Copper River Reds from The **Copper River**, east of **Mile 1350***

ICY BAY HIGH SCHOOL

A few year's back I got an Icy Bay High School graduation card from a friend's son. It had a school logo and certainly looked like the real deal. But then I got to thinking: the only things in Icy Bay were a small fishing lodge, and a logging camp that I thought was closed up.. no way were there enough kids for a high school...

A little later I bumped into my friend and asked her about her son and the card.

"There isn't any high school," said she, "Our son is the caretaker of the logging camp, they're the only family there. They're homeschooling the kids. They just thought he should have a graduation card like the real ones so they printed one up."

Exploring:
The Hidden Jewel: Prince William Sound

The hidden jewel of Prince William Sound is College Fjord. Within an eight- mile stretch at the upper end, five major tidewater glaciers reach the water.

While Glacier Bay emerged from the ice so recently that big trees haven't grown up close to the ice, College Fjord is a place where the forest and the glaciers have co-existed for centuries.

This is also the place where you are most likely to see sea otters. A good place to look is on top of ice floes, where you may see them with their young.

Above: massive Harvard Glacier at the head of Prince William Sound.

*Right: sea otter in classic pose - swimming on his back.*DK

Lower right: this ice cave is probably 60-80' high, judging from the trees on left.

Below: 60' high spruce trees give an idea of the size of Wellesley Glacier.

On a calm March evening in 1983, the big tanker Exxon Valdez collided with a well marked reef and spilled some 11 million gallons of heavy crude oil.

It was a major blow to commercial salmon fishermen as the oil moved west, closing commercial fishing areas as it passed.

*North of **Mile 1480** is the **Columbia Glacier**, the fastest retreating glacier in Alaska, moving back around 90 feet a day in 1981, and **calving almost 2 cubic miles of ice a year**. The Exxon Valdez was dodging ice from this glacier when it hit the rock.*

Exploring:
Chiswell Islands

INTO THE GREAT SEA CAVE

Once I was a guest lecturer/naturalist aboard this small (100 passenger) cruise ship and we stopped at the Chiswell Islands, part of the Alaska Maritime Wildlife Refuge, west of Seward.

Mildred was a sprightly lady, whose family had brought from a nursing home in Maine, to be with them on this trip. 90 years old or not, she wanted to go on every adventure, every excursion.

But on the day we visited the Chiswells, there was a long swell running, making it awkward, borderline dangerous, for us to get aboard the big Zodiac inflatables for the excursion. I tried to point out the danger, but Mildred was having none of it, and so the Filipino crew waited for the right moment, grabbed her, and plunked her down safely aboard.

When we got close to the islands, the big swell was just booming into the sea caves, throwing spray far and wide.

"C'mon, Joe," Mildred said, "Take us into the sea cave."

"Mildred," said I, "That'd be too dangerous; we'd be smooshed.."

"I know," said she, "but that's so much better than wasting away in the nursing home..."

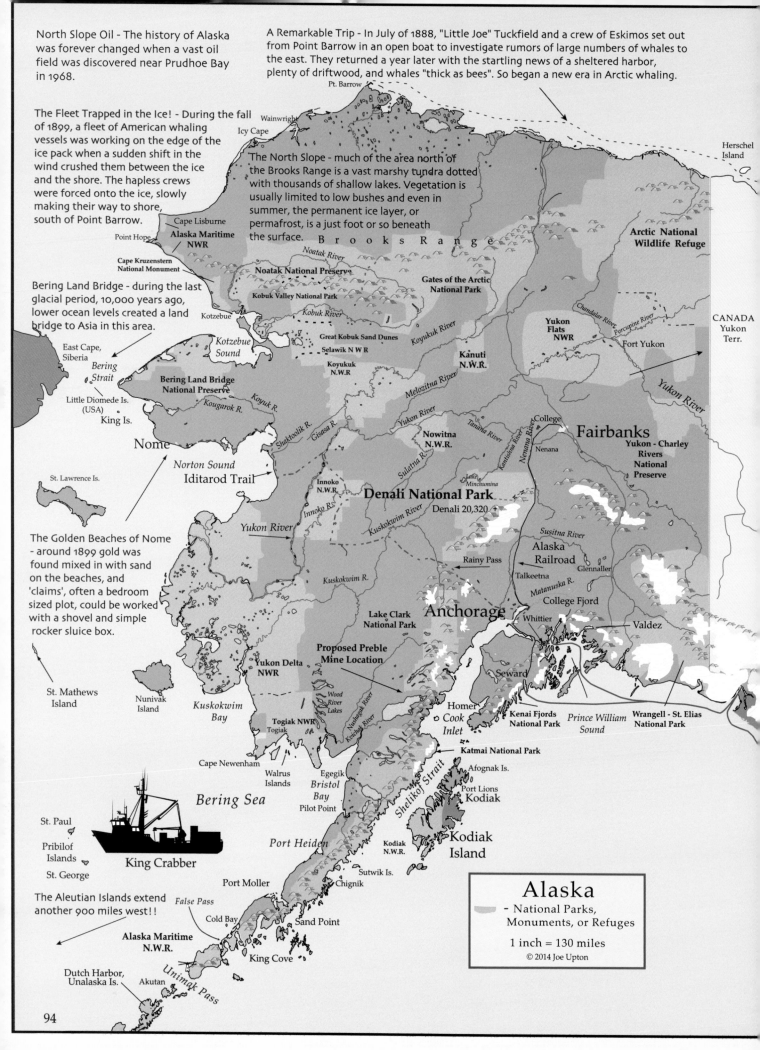

North Slope Oil - The history of Alaska was forever changed when a vast oil field was discovered near Prudhoe Bay in 1968.

A Remarkable Trip - In July of 1888, "Little Joe" Tuckfield and a crew of Eskimos set out from Point Barrow in an open boat to investigate rumors of large numbers of whales to the east. They returned a year later with the startling news of a sheltered harbor, plenty of driftwood, and whales "thick as bees". So began a new era in Arctic whaling.

The Fleet Trapped in the Ice! - During the fall of 1899, a fleet of American whaling vessels was working on the edge of the ice pack when a sudden shift in the wind crushed them between the ice and the shore. The hapless crews were forced onto the ice, slowly making their way to shore, south of Point Barrow.

The North Slope - much of the area north of the Brooks Range is a vast marshy tundra dotted with thousands of shallow lakes. Vegetation is usually limited to low bushes and even in summer, the permanent ice layer, or permafrost, is a just foot or so beneath the surface.

Bering Land Bridge - during the last glacial period, 10,000 years ago, lower ocean levels created a land bridge to Asia in this area.

The Golden Beaches of Nome - around 1899 gold was found mixed in with sand on the beaches, and 'claims', often a bedroom sized plot, could be worked with a shovel and simple rocker sluice box.

The Aleutian Islands extend another 900 miles west!!

Pt. Barrow
Wainwright
Icy Cape
Herschel Island
Cape Lisburne
Point Hope
Alaska Maritime NWR
Cape Kruzenstern National Monument
B r o o k s   R a n g e
Arctic National Wildlife Refuge
Noatak River
Noatak National Preserve
Kobuk Valley National Park
Gates of the Arctic National Park
Kotzebue
Kobuk River
Chandalar River
Porcupine River
CANADA Yukon Terr.
Great Kobuk Sand Dunes
Selawik N W R
Koyukuk River
Yukon Flats NWR
Fort Yukon
East Cape, Siberia
Kotzebue Sound
Koyukuk N.W.R
Kanuti N.W.R.
Bering Strait
Little Diomede Is. (USA)
King Is.
Bering Land Bridge National Preserve
Kougarok R.
Koyuk R.
Melozitna River
Yukon River
Shaktoolik R.
Gisasa R.
Yukon River
Suliatna R.
Tanana River
Nowitna N.W.R.
College
Fairbanks
Nome
Norton Sound
Iditarod Trail
Kantishna River
Nenana River
Nenana
Yukon - Charley Rivers National Preserve
St. Lawrence Is.
Innoko N.W.R.
Lake Minchumina
Denali National Park
Denali 20,320 +
Innoko Rs.
Yukon River
Kuskokwim River
Susitna River
Alaska Railroad
Rainy Pass
Talkeetna
Glennaller
Kuskokwim R.
Matanuska R.
College Fjord
St. Mathews Island
Nunivak Island
Kuskokwim Bay
Yukon Delta NWR
Proposed Preble Mine Location
Lake Clark National Park
Anchorage
Whittier
Valdez
Seward
Kenai Fjords National Park
Prince William Sound
Wrangell - St. Elias National Park
Wood River Lakes
Togiak NWR
Togiak
Nushagak River
Kvichak River
Homer
Cook Inlet
Katmai National Park
Cape Newenham
Walrus Islands
Egegik
Bristol Bay
Pilot Point
Shelikof Strait
Afognak Is.
Port Lions
Kodiak
St. Paul
Pribilof Islands
St. George
Bering Sea
King Crabber
Port Heiden
Kodiak N.W.R.
Sutwik Is.
Chignik
Kodiak Island
Port Moller
False Pass
Cold Bay
Sand Point
Alaska Maritime N.W.R.
Dutch Harbor, Unalaska Is.
Akutan
King Cove
Unimak Pass

Alaska
- National Parks, Monuments, or Refuges

1 inch = 130 miles

© 2014 Joe Upton

THE VASTNESS:
WESTERN ALASKA

Western Alaska is mostly roadless. Travel is by plane, boat, snowmobile, and even dogsled occasionally. The invention of the snowmobile around 1960 transformed winter transportation in much of The North. Before snowmobiles, many Natives in remote areas had to keep large teams of dogs, catch and dry fish to feed them, and take care of them for the rest of the year in order to have them for winter travel.

The land is dotted with tiny Native communities. Life is often a struggle with income from seasonal construction jobs and fishing often not enough to last through the long winter.

A very large part of this land is tundra—wide areas of spongy wetland dotted by shallow ponds. In the darkness of the long winters, all this land sleeps. But the Arctic spring begins an awakening process that transforms The North.

The great flyways bring millions of migrating birds to the vast delta country of the Yukon, Kuskokwim, and smaller rivers. The long days cause vegetation of all sorts to grow at a rate not seen elsewhere.

Top: Aniachak Volcano with its steam vent looms over the Ugashik River. Many of these volcanoes are active. When I was a king crab fisherman working on the Bering Sea after dark, sometimes an eruption would fill the sky, seen just by us crab fishermen, and a few hundred natives.

Right, middle: Coffee Point Airport on the Egegik River in Bristol Bay. In such places, aviation gasoline is often delivered in drums by barge in the spring. The plane is a Piper Super Cub with tundra tires, probably used for spotting fish.

Right, bottom: Part of the endless tundra.

Twice the size of Long Island, but with a population of just 14,000 souls, Kodiak Island is big and wild. With substantial salmon runs, commercial fishing was the first big industry and still is.

Home to the Sugpiaq tribe of Alaska natives, they were fishermen and hunters until the Russian's arrival around 1884. With an insatiable hunger for sea otter pelts, the Russians subjugated the natives in pretty brutal fashion, forcing them to hunt otters. After Russia sold Alaska to the United States in 1867, Kodiak was, due to its remoteness, only slowly settled by Americans, primarily coming to fish and raise foxes for their fur. Salmon canneries, each due to its remoteness, having to be a whole little town in itself, popped up in many bays around the island.

But the fishery that put Kodiak on the map, was king crab, now celebrated in the Discovery Channel series, Deadliest Catch. Today's boats are steel with impressive modern electronics and hydraulics; but in the early days it was wooden boats and tough, tough men. When the 200 mile limit was enacted in 1976 pushing the big foreign fleets out of the Bering Sea, Kodiak fishermen were among the first to get in on what was to become legendary fishing, with crew shares on top boats approaching 100,000$ in the late 70s and early 1980s.

Tourism, centered primarily on sportsfishing, is also a significant part of the Kodiak summer economy.

Top: king crab and happy crewman, 1971. This fellow, Walter Kuhr, started out as a deckhand in 1971, and within a decade was owner of several big crabbing and trawling boats. His story was not uncommon.

Right: where there's salmon, there are usually bears not too far away. At waterfalls, the alpha male gets the best spot, where he can actually catch jumping salmon with his teeth. When he's got one, he will walk over to the bank, put one hand on the fish's head, neatly strip off a fillet with his claw, flip the fish over to fillet the other side, and just flip the carcass to the gulls.

Above: Russian Orthodox cross on grave - the influence of the Russians is still very visible around the island.

Left: wooden king crabber, circa 1960. This style of boat was built originally as a sardine seiner in California, and not really suited for the rigors of the Alaska coast in winter. But, the price was right, so many ended up as crabbers in the early years.

97

VOICES FROM DENALI

"...The storm now became so severe that I was actually afraid to get new dry mittens out of my rucksack, for I knew my hands would be frozen in the process... The last period of our climb is like the memory of an evil dream. La Voy was completely lost in the ice mist, and Professor Parker's frosted form was an indistinct blur above me... The breath was driven from my body and I held to my axe with stooped shoulders to stand against the gale; I couldn't go ahead. As I brushed the frost from my glasses and squinted upward through the stinging snow, I saw a sight that will haunt me to my dying day. The slope above me was no longer steep! That was all I could see. What it meant I will never know for certain—all I can say is that we were close to the top."

— Belmore Browne, *The Conquest of Mt. McKinley*

"I was snowshoeing along about fifty feet back of the sled, with Harry (Liek) right behind me when, without warning, the snow fell away under my snowshoes. I plunged into sudden darkness.

"I had time to let out a feeble shout. Then for a couple of long, long seconds I plummeted downward. I remember thinking, 'This is it, fellow!' Then my pack scraped against the side of the crevasse, my head banged hard against the ice wall, and I came to a jarring stop.

"When my head cleared and I could look around in the blue darkness, I saw I was on a plug of snow wedged between the ice walls. On either side, this wedge of snow fell away into sheer blackness.

"About forty feet above me I could see a ray of sunlight, slanting through the hole I had made in the surface crust. The crevasse was about twelve feet wide up there, it narrowed to two feet down where I was. Below was icy death."

— Grant Pearson, *My Life of High Adventure*

Top: Denali, 1932. When we look at the high tech equipment today's climbers consider essential, our respect for the pioneer climbers grows.
Above right : Harry Liek and Alfred Lindley after the climb. Liek was Superintendent of Mt. Mckinley National Park. UAF Rasmusen Library photos.

TRAGEDY ON THE MOUNTAIN

Members of the 1932 Lindley - Liek Expedition, returning from the first successful climb to both summits, found an empty camp. It belonged to Theodore Koven and Alan Carpe, who had been flown onto Muldrow Glacier by legendary pilot Joe Crosson. The pair were there to make cosmic ray observations and were thrilled that Crosson had been able to make the first glacier landing on Denali to drop them.

Exploring nearby, the members of the Lindley - Liek Expedition, already exhausted by climbing for almost 36 hours straight, found Koven's frozen body. Footprints indicated that Koven and Carp had probably fallen through the snow into a crevasse, and that Koven, unable to rescue his partner, managed to climb out, but succumbed to his injuries and perished from hypothermia.

"There was no pride of conquest.... Rather...that a privileged communion with the high places of the earth had been granted... secret and solitary since the world began. All the way down, unconscious of weariness in the descent, my thoughts were occupied with the glorious scene my eyes gazed upon, and should gaze upon never again."

First coming to Alaska as an eight-year old on a sightseeing trip, Belmore Browne became an important figure in Alaska climbing as well as a significant wildlife painter.

Browne was part of the 1906 Denali expedition when the leader, Frederick Cook, sent his crew away, and claimed to have reached the top solo.

Browne doubted that he had and went on another expedition four years later that found that Cook's photographic "proof" was in fact of another peak, 20 miles away from Denali.

As the quote on the left reveals, Browne came very very close (about 125') to the top on his third attempt in 1912. ASL PCA 01-3441

"But in half an hour, we stood on the narrow edge of the spur top, facing failure. Here, where the black ridge leading to the tops of the pink cliffs should have flattened, all was absolutely sheer, and a hanging glacier, bearded and dripping with bergschrunds, filled the angle in between... I heard Fred say, 'It ain't that we can't find a way that's possible, taking chances. There ain't no way.'

"We were checkmated with steepness, at 11,300 feet with eight days of mountain food on our hands. But remember this: also with scarce two weeks provisions below with which to reach the coast and winter coming. The foolishness of the situation, and the fascination, lies in the fact that except in this fair weather, unknown in Alaska at this season, we might have perished either night in those two exposed camps."
— Robert Dunn, *Shameless Diary of an Explorer*

"We tried to take some snaps, but had to give it up. For four minutes only did I leave my mittens off, and in that time, I froze five tips of my fingers to such a degree that after they had first been white, some weeks later, they turned black, and at last fell off, with the nails and all."
— Erling Strom, *How We Climbed Mt. McKinley*

"... My mind was racing. I had to grab the rock near Dave with my left hand; it was bare, no mitten or sock. It would be frozen. I had to. Suddenly my bare hand shot out to grab the rock. Slicing cold.

"I saw Dave's face, the end of his nose raw, frostbitten. His mouth, distorted into an agonized mixture of compassion and anger, swore at me to get a glove on. I looked at my hand. It was white, frozen absolutely white."
–Art Davidson, *Minus 148°, the Winter Ascent of Mt. McKinley*

Top quote by Hudson Stuck, in Mt. McKinley: The Pioneer Climbs *by Terris Moore*

ON THE GREAT RIVERS

Norh and west of Fairbanks is the vast Alaska bush. This is river country. The majority of villages and settlements in the region between the Alaska Range and the Bering Sea and Arctic Ocean lie along one of the many rivers with Native and Russian names like Kitchatna, Tonzona, Kantishna, Hoholitna, and Chilikadrotna, Ugashik, Nushagak, and Kinak. When the sea ice recedes from shore during the summer, watercraft ranging from big tugs and barges to outboard jet boats move people and supplies around. When the ice is in, it is usually hard and smooth enough for vehicles.

Where there are no highways, the arrival of the first freight barge in the spring is always an exciting community event. This freight (usually in 40-foot containers or vans) often begins its journey from Seattle, stacked five and six high on a huge 400-foot ocean-going barge, towed by a 5,000-horsepower tug. Somewhere near the mouth of the Yukon River, perhaps at St. Michaels, the containers are hoisted onto a smaller barge, to be pushed upstream. Sometimes, for freight bound for villages on the smaller rivers, the container would be transferred a third time onto a yet smaller barge, pushed by an even smaller tug.

"Ice Out," before air travel, was a big event. Notices were posted around towns like Fairbanks to keep residents informed: "Ice moved at Fort Gibbon this morning at 8 a.m." This was important news because movement upriver of the first steamer of the season meant fresh vegetables, followed shortly thereafter by the "slaughterhouse boat" with its pens of cows, sheep, pigs, geese, and chickens brought up from Seattle.

Top: paddlewheelers pulled up on the shore for the winter around 1910. Moving ice scoured the riverbanks, so boats were pulled up competely out of reach of the water and ice. UW Nowell 6037

Opposite page: Inside an old gold dredge, which were seen on many Alaska rivers Above: Float planes are the aerial equivalents of pickup trucks for many bush Alaskans.

Right: somewhere on the lower Yukon, a small steam paddlewheeler loads freight headed for the smaller communities along the Kobuk River. UW Nowell 112

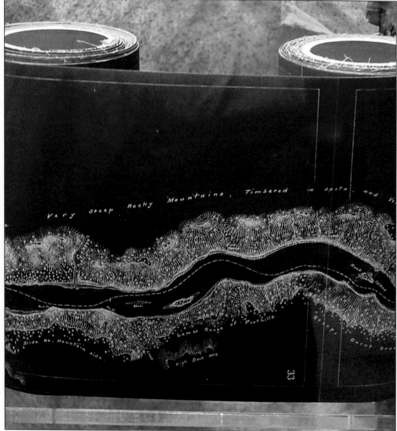

Top: Passengers leaving the steamer Tutsi *at Ben-My-Chree, on the Upper Yukon, circa 1925.*

Left: River channels changed frequently, so hand-drawn charts were created by the paddlewheeler captains and river pilots. This one of much of the river is taped together from many sheets, rolled back or forth as the trip demands.

Opposite page, top: Steamers would operate as late as possible each fall. Once the rivers froze, there would be little income for months. Sometimes a steamer such as this one would stay too late, becoming frozen in the ice. Yukon Archives

Opposite page, bottom: The steamer White Horse *moving upriver in Five Finger Rapids on the Upper Yukon. This was a particularly challenging spot. Because the rapids were narrow and the current heavy, steamers needed plenty of power to get through. Under-powered vessels would run a line to shore and winch themselves through, aided by the paddlewheels turning at full speed ahead. This was the route used by the majority of the men who headed north to the Klondike Gold Rush in 1898. Only the wealthy could afford steamer passage with all their gear. Most built their own boats and floated down the river.* UW21255

Before the arrival of modern social services and the cash economy, winters in the far north could be another word for starvation if game was scarce.

In those days, the sea and land provided a hard living. The result was a remarkably tough and resilient people. In boats made of walrus hides stitched together and stretched over driftwood frames, they traveled hundreds of miles to hunt bowhead and other whales. Other hunters waited for hours by holes in the ice for a seal to surface briefly to breathe.

Housing was sod and earth huts, or igloos in winter, and skin tents when families moved to be closer to fish runs in the summer. When the white men came, Eskimos quickly learned about commerce and the value of their ivory carvings. As soon as the gold rush created settlements of whites in western Alaska, Eskimos began to camp nearby to carve and sell ivory.

Today's Eskimos are more apt to live in prefab houses delivered by barge and depend on seasonal fishing and construction work.

Camp

Ken Lisbourne
Pt. Hope, Alaska

Above: "Summer Camp," *a painting by Ken Lisbourne, Point Hope. Often Eskimos, especially those living near the deltas of the great Yukon and Kuskokwim rivers, would travel to campsites on the water where they could catch salmon and set up drying racks. In addition to preserving fish for themselves, they would often dry many chum salmon to feed their dog teams over the winter.* Author's collection

Right: Yu'pik Ircit, or human/fox mask, from the author's collection. Eskimo legend has it that Ircenrrat were extraordinary persons who appeared alternately as humans or small mammals. This would be revealed as footprints that would alternate between animal and human tracks.

Opposite page, top: "Shoppers" *aboard a trading schooner, circa 1920. Each year, trading vessels would travel north to Bering Sea Eskimo villages loaded with supplies such as sewing machines, five-gallon tins of kerosene, Aladdin Lamps, fabric, rifles, and all manner of smaller items. Natives like these women would come aboard with skins or ivory to trade for supplies.* UW17962

Opposite page, bottom: Ivory Carvers during the Nome Gold Rush. UW17963

THE UNFRIENDLY BERING SEA

The farther west you go, the bleaker the land becomes. In the Aleutians, trees bigger than a human are rarely seen. On the mainland, the land is mostly tundra and ponds, backed up by austere volcanoes. On the eastern shore of the Bering Sea, good harbors are few; the shores are all scoured by the ice pack in winter, threatening docks and breakwaters. But underneath lies a rich fisheries resource that has been harvested by many nations for decades.

In deeper waters father offshore lie king crab, target of the "Deadliest Catch" fleet. Imposed by Congress in 1976, the 200-mile limit first allowed joint ventures: US boats fishing for foreign processor ships, and eventually this led to the development of sophisticated, high-tech U.S. fishing vessels such as the one above.

In the 1980's it was essentially a new gold rush as entrepreneurs rushed to get big ships built to operate in the new fisheries. Regulations were quickly put in place to control overfishing.

Ironically, the biggest money is made with the tiny roe sacs of the lowly pollock. A large fleet of large vessels has been developed for this fishery.

The hard part is simply that the Bering Sea is rough, dangerous, and cold for much of the year.

Top: Aleutian fun: a 300-foot trawler/processor, Bering Sea, 2013, blowing probably 60 knots. Tony Norg
Left, this vessel sank after heavy seas broke loose a heavy crab pot, which in turn broke off the air vent to one of the vessel's compartments. Seas sweeping across the deck filled the compartment.
Bottom left: Rough weather on our crabber, the Flood Tide, *Bering Sea, 1971*

A hundred thirty years after the first cannery was built on Bristol Bay in the eastern Bering Sea, the Bay's fishery is still going strong. The few old-timers who still remember the sailboat days, a time prior to 1950 when only sailing vessels were allowed to fish the bay, shake their heads in wonder at what they see now.

Today, thanks to the 200-mile limit that kept foreign fleets from targeting U.S. Bristol Bay salmon, this is the strongest red salmon fishery in the world. But it's short and very intense. Each June, some 10,000 fishermen and 5,000 processing workers arrive to work the six-week season. The peak of the season lasts only about ten days, amid pressure to be in the right spot and keep your equipment and crew working. A good day fishing in the right place can represent ten percent of your catch for the entire season.

Top: Sailboat days—lines of sailing gillnetters being towed back from the fishing grounds. Pulling the nets by hand, rowing with 14-foot oars, and sailing in the choppy waters of the bay was tough work.

Right, middle: Intense action on "the line." Fishing areas are tightly regulated and boats fight to be right here where fish pour into the bay.

Right, bottom: Picking red salmon aboard your mapmaker's gillnetter, 1995. On the right is our son, Matthew, now a maritime lawyer.

EFFECTS OF A CHANGING CLIMATE

It's completely beyond what any of our models had predicted."

"I never expected it to melt this fast."

Such were the comments from scientists at a recent symposium on the Arctic. There still may be debate in a few quarters about global warming, but not in Alaska—it's here.

The tidewater glaciers on the Alaska coast had been receding slowly for decades, even before global warming became a household word. But recent events in the Arctic and their implications for the future are sobering, especially for species dependent on wide areas of sea ice such as the polar bear.

Until a decade or so ago, sea ice covered most of the Arctic Ocean in winter, melting and receding a bit in the summer, and then refreezing quickly again each fall. But recently the sea ice has receded dramatically in the summer. From 1979 to 2000, the average area of ice in the Arctic Ocean was around three million square miles. By August of 2007, that number had shrunk by half, a truly staggering reduction. One scientist predicted that the Arctic would be ice free in summer by 2030.

It may happen sooner. As ice melts, the darker ocean absorbs much more heat than the white ice which reflects the sun's rays, further increasing the melting.

The climate change will create losers and winners. The Northwest Passage shipping route from Atlantic to Pacific would become reality. New areas would be open for mineral and oil exploration. Valuable fish species such as salmon and pollock might thrive by moving their range farther north. The polar bear would probably be a loser, depending on the ice pack for habitat.

Many Native villages in the Arctic are built close to the shore, but had been protected from storm seas by a natural barrier created by the ice. As the ice recedes, the seas become larger, and villages may either have to relocate or eventually be swept away. Permafrost–frozen earth close to the surface of the ground is another huge issue. Most small buildings and houses in the Arctic essentially have permafrost foundations. As the ice in soil melts, the buildings slowly settle into the soggy ground.

Can global warming be stopped? In theory, perhaps. But the realities of a rapidly developing Asia and a global economy built on high energy use make it unlikely.

So, if you want to see Alaska in its present state, go soon! *Alaskastock Photo*

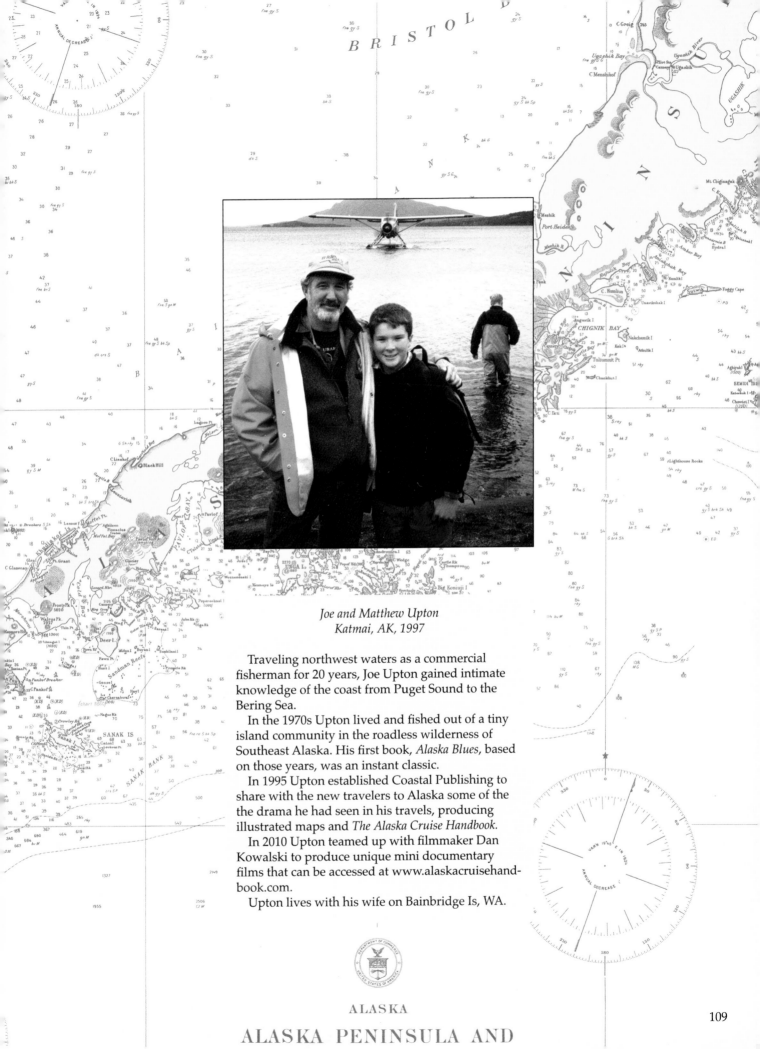

Joe and Matthew Upton
Katmai, AK, 1997

Traveling northwest waters as a commercial fisherman for 20 years, Joe Upton gained intimate knowledge of the coast from Puget Sound to the Bering Sea.

In the 1970s Upton lived and fished out of a tiny island community in the roadless wilderness of Southeast Alaska. His first book, *Alaska Blues*, based on those years, was an instant classic.

In 1995 Upton established Coastal Publishing to share with the new travelers to Alaska some of the the drama he had seen in his travels, producing illustrated maps and *The Alaska Cruise Handbook*.

In 2010 Upton teamed up with filmmaker Dan Kowalski to produce unique mini documentary films that can be accessed at www.alaskacruisehand-book.com.

Upton lives with his wife on Bainbridge Is, WA.

ALASKA

ALASKA PENINSULA AND

ARCTIC

ASIA

GULF OF
ANADIR

BEHRING
SEA

Government Station W Point Barrow
Smith B.
Hal

C. Lisburne

Pt. Hope W

Ikpikpung R.
Meade R.
Colville R.

KOTZEBUE
SOUND

Noatak R.

Ft Morton

Jade Mts
3500
Koo-wak R.

Selawik R.

Nogahik Kakat R.
KŎYUKUK R.

East Cape

BEHRING STRAIT.

Cape
Prince
of Wales
Teller's Reindeer Station
Port Clarende W

Indian Pt.

ST. LAWRENCE ID.

C. Nome

C. DARBY

Norton Bay

Nulato

Walasatux

Mt. Nanonlak

Welozi Kakat. R.
Nowrickset
Palisades

Noothakat R.
Klatsilagitat R.

NORTON SOUND

Shaktolik
Eqowik

C. Denbigh

Unalaklik

Aurakakat

YUKON RIV.

Kaltag
Kayuh R.

St. Michael
E99.I
ST. MICHAEL
Stuart I.

Minik R.
Mink R.
Trail

BEHRING SEA

Mouths of the
YUKON RIVER.

C. Dyer
C. Romanz.

Kusilvak

C. Mohican

Nunivak I.

Etolin Strait

Pastolik

Kutlik

Anvik

Holy Cross Mission
Andreafska
Igomut

Koserafski

RedoubtKolmakof

Oknagamut

Odgavamut
Gavigamut

Kuskokwim R.

North For
Toyona
West Forelan

ALAS

Nikhkak
Lake
11277 ft
Redoubt Vol.
Iliamna Peak
12066

Bethel

Quinehaha

Avigarik
Hakavik

Nuchagak R.

Iliamna Lake

Warehouse

COOKS

Port Graha
C. Elizabe

C. Newenham

Anagnakl
Ft. Alexander

BRISTOL BAY

SHELIKOF STRAIT

ROUTE OF THE PACIFIC STEAM WHALING COS. WHALING STEAMERS

ALASKA PENINSULA

PACIFIC STEAM WHALING COS

Chignic

C

Coal
Sandpoint

Unimak Isle.

Unimak Pass

TRINITY IS.

KADIAK ID.

CA

Dutch Harbor

UNALASKA
ID.

110

1915 Map prepared by whaling company, showing
their ship routes as well as gold deposits, etc.

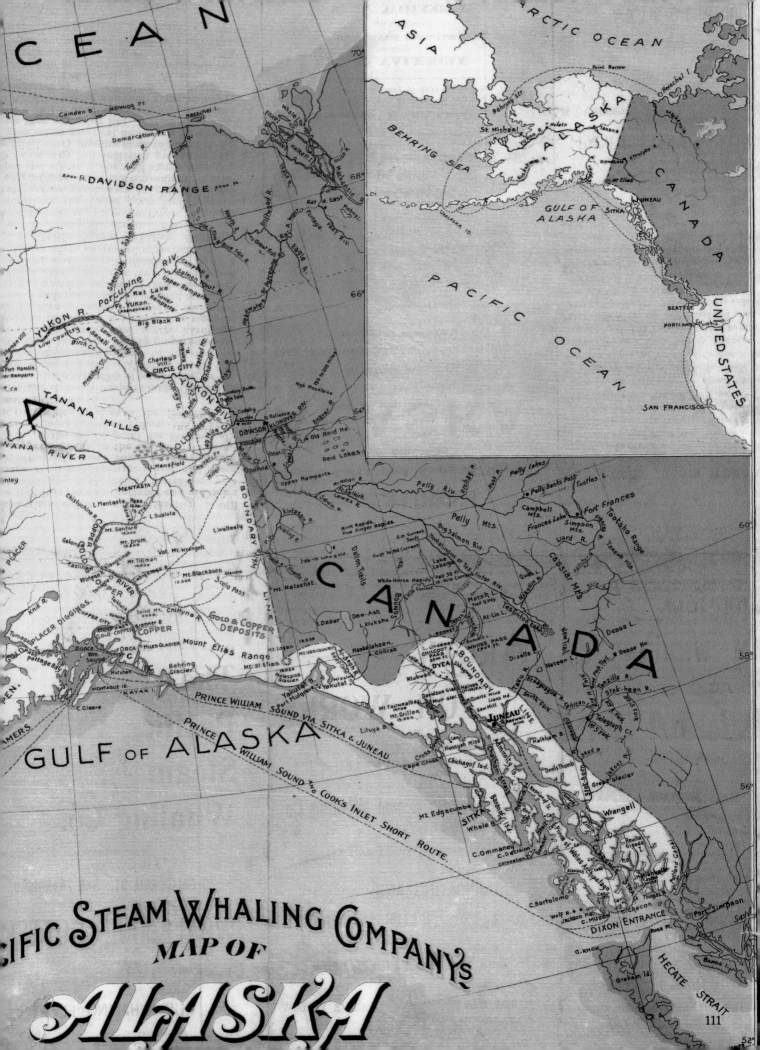

PACIFIC STEAM WHALING COMPANYS MAP OF ALASKA

111

This 1918 Post Office route map shows the challenges of getting the mail around western Alaska. The winter routes are by dog sled, and the summer routes by steamboat or horseback. This map is one of many at: www.historicalcharts.noaa.gov.